ECONOMIC THEORY

Dr. John Henry Wadley III, Ph.D.

authorHOUSE®

AuthorHouse™
1663 Liberty Drive
Bloomington, IN 47403
www.authorhouse.com
Phone: 1-800-839-8640

First published by AuthorHouse   04/05/2011

ISBN: 978-1-4567-6489-0 (e)
ISBN: 978-1-4567-6490-6 (hc)
ISBN: 978-1-4567-6491-3 (sc)

Library of Congress Control Number: 2011906082

Printed in the United States of America

Any people depicted in stock imagery provided by Thinkstock are models,
and such images are being used for illustrative purposes only.
Certain stock imagery © Thinkstock.

This book is printed on acid-free paper.

Contents

INTRODUCTION

What is "commerce" and what effect does it have on our daily lives? Everything we do, everything we buy to sustain our health, happiness or sense of contentment involves transactions with others. It is axiomatic that in order to possess the goods others are selling or to obtain the skills or services someone else can provide, there must be a meaningful transaction to compensate the provider of the desired good or service. This procurement or trading of one material good or service for another has been taking place since before recorded history.

Also part of history is the distortion of commerce. Though the most obvious factors such as theft, war and taxation have played a significant role in hampering pure trade, there are other, more subtle factors and influences that are rarely discussed; yet have played an integral part in the worst events of human history. These influences, such as credit, interest, and "fiat money" are deemed "subtle" in the sense that the masses do not recognize the destructive forces behind them. Out in the open, seemingly common, acceptable practices such as mortgages and money based on nothing but "the full faith and credit" of a given entity, give rise to complacency. In reality, the unsuspecting public has fallen victim to practices and procedures that, in the past, has led to recessions, depressions, wars, famine, and enslavement of populations.

In the midst of those who produce and those who procure the goods and services are the merchants, the money-changers (banks), and the law merchants. Those who "facilitate" the transactions neither add value to the wanted goods or services, nor do they generate anything of value themselves. Instead, they would argue, they add convenience so that more transactions can occur, helping everyone get what they want and exacting only a small price for their services. However, it can be shown that the merchant, banking and legal classes -- through intentional design, i.e., the law of commerce, civil law and maritime law -- have created a system that benefits only themselves to the detriment of those who actually produce goods or provide service.

Unless we fully understand the ramification of the events around us and become mindful of not only the systems of government and businesses, but also what they are doing any why; we are destined to fall into the same traps as our forefathers. In addition, unless and until we become responsible for our own welfare and learn to depend upon ourselves by living within our means, we are subject the same fate of the failed cultures that came before us.

Throughout history there is a common thread that weaves together societies, businesses, governments, and the rise and fall of great civilizations. That thread is commerce. It is true that wealth and the ability to accumulate wealth has not only been the driving force behind great expansions and technological advances, but it has also been the cause of economic disaster, hardship, and the fall of empires. It has been capital (however defined at any specific moment in history) that was, and continues to be, the driving force behind the means of production. But, unfortunately, the distortion of trade and commerce is not only allowed for by law, but promoted by businesses, banks, lawyers and politicians as well. Thus, commerce in its present form has become the vehicle of self-destruction. We are currently living within a system that will create a two-tiered social structure: The 2% who own and control everything and everyone else, who own absolutely nothing and die in debt, which will subsequently bind their children to the same financial/economic slavery.

It has been, and continues to be, intervention into pure commerce through the promulgation of usurious laws (allowing for loans, interest and credit) which has always distorted trade and commerce. These laws, rules, and regulations favor only certain segments and classes of society and prevent the masses from ever obtaining economic freedom. As repeated often in the course of human history, these legal and political structures have resulted in the world's greatest upheavals and man-made disasters. Yet, we as a society not only allow it, but fully participate in it, to our own detriment.

This is not in any way to say that commerce is bad. It does however, say that commerce brings with it the laws of commerce. Wherever commerce goes, it brings laws that bind people into slavery. It is important to understand that this can happen only if people agree with it, support it and participate in it. The leaders of society, whether it be dictators, emperors or elected officials, become enamored with wealth and power. Using the facade of politics, they pass the laws which enables them, and those who offer them more wealth and power, to control all trade. They promote instruments such as mortgages, credit cards and insurance products that perpetually have the masses in debt. It is through these laws that the merchant class, the money-lenders, and the law brokers subjugate the masses. Entire societies have, and continue to, act passively, unknowingly, and blindly empowering the same people who seek to keep them in perpetual chains of poverty.

In this chapter, we will explore the history of commerce, the way different societies and religions have described commerce through the ages, and the influence commerce has had on diverse societies. In addition, we will explore how segments of the population use laws, political maneuvers and business structures to distort commerce -- all to the detriment of the people.

THE HISTORY OF COMMERCE

It is important to know and understand history so that we do not fall victim to the same mistakes of the past. Because most people are ignorant of the past, they do not realize they are following the same path countless others have followed, nor where that path leads. By becoming familiar with the events of the past, knowing the reasons why powerful empires failed, why countries went to war, and how the masses have suffered for the benefit of the powerful few, an informed individual can avoid this same fate.

History can tell us where we are heading if we continue to follow the lead of our elected officials, rely on their economic house of cards or conduct our affairs as promoted and expected by the true power-brokers: the merchants, bankers and lawyers. Through knowledge and recognition of the true nature of commerce, the legal system and politics the masses can avoid the same fate as countless other past civilizations. What it comes down to is personal responsibility with enough courage and forethought to not accept the status quo. It takes courage to expose the "power brokers" and reject their system of commerce. In order to exact change, the masses must refuse to participate in credit based commerce and demand an end to the creation of wealth based on nothing. There is only one reason these societal and personal economic disasters occur. It is because we, the masses, allow it and we, as individuals, continually fail to act responsibly. This same scenario has happened for more than 4000 years.

The value in looking at the past is to uncover movements of men during other ages; where their behavior in similar settings are known. Then, the true nature and the real intent behind the influential men of today can be exposed.

"If we consider the shortness of human life, and our limited knowledge even of what passes in our lifetime, we must be sensible that we should be forever children of understanding, were it not for this invention, which extends our experience to all past ages and to our improvement in wisdom as they had actually laid under our observation. A man acquainted with history may in some respect, be said to have lived from the beginning of the world, and to have been making continual additions to his stock of knowledge in every country."

David Hume: London of the Study of History, page 390 (1898)

The relevance of documented events of ancient times, using sources such as the Bible, will become apparent. Although not as reliable as a present-day, well-documented thesis, the discussions of the subject matter the ancient people chose to preserve is quite revealing. From the oldest, most reliable sources, we can learn that the way our law and society is structured is not new or novel.

History of Law Structure in America - Genesis to Present Time

IN THE BEGINNING

The Book of Genesis has been translated from Samarian scripts that have been unearthed only decades ago in recently discovered Nineveh and other areas of the Tigris/Euphrates area in the Middle East. These ancient scripts recorded on baked clay tablets date back to a civilization that was highly educated, incredibly organized and socially advanced. These scriptures date back to as far as 4000 B.C.

2123 BC - Abraham, grandfather of the Israelites, was originally from the ancient city of Nippur and later moved to Ur (both major cities of Sumer)

2023 BC - Isaac, son of Abraham, is born (Genesis 21:)

2000 BC - Babylon flourishes in the land of Sumer (Shinar).

It is very important to realize and understand the roots of our social structures. Based on archaeological discoveries, we now know that what we think of as new or modern, is simply a continuation of the ways of the past. Babylon had a modern system of life with canals to irrigate their land for agriculture, indoor toilets, city sewage systems and public restrooms. They also had a city to city postal system using baked clay letters and envelopes.

Moreover, Babylon had a judicial system where judges wore black robes, just as they do today. Studying Babylonian society from thousands of years ago reveals that the concepts, ideas and systems we have adopted were not sprouted from the minds of brilliant men just a few hundred years ago; but instead are much older than we imagine.

Babylon eventually fell victim to their own greed. As has happened over and over again though the ages, those in power of the most advanced, successful civilization of that time expanded beyond their capability to rule and govern. The exacted a heavy price in terms of human and material resources on the peoples they conquered. Instead of ruling and governing for the benefit of the people, the ruling class, the priests and the other "elites" of that time, subjugated the masses for their own gain. Bowing to their idols of gold and silver, they eventually began to fall into disgrace but continued to rule through fiction until they were destroyed. It was their desire for more material, more possessions, and more control of trade and commerce throughout the known world that led to their collapse, as the people of other nation-states, other cultures, rejected their ways, grew more powerful and fought back.

Some of the systems in place in Ancient Babylon that survive to this day include coined money (banks), receipts, title seals, signing and merchant law. It was their development of merchant law and the systems of controlling commerce which evolved into Roman Law, then into Civil Law and later became Maritime Law.

1963 BC - Jacob (Israel is born). (Genesis 25:26)

1890 BC - Joseph, Jacob's son, sold into slavery to Egypt. (Genesis 37:2)

1833 BC - Israel sojourns into Egypt because of famine. (Genesis 15:13)

1513 BC - Israel becomes slaves to Egypt and Moses is born.

1433 BC - Exodus of Israel out of Egypt through the Red Sea and into the wilderness.

1432 BC - God gives Moses the Ten Commandments to give to Israel (Exodus 20)

1393 BC - Israel reaches Promised Land and Moses dies.

953 BC - Solomon starts building temple at Jerusalem. (Kings 6:1)

587 BC - Nebuchadnezzar, King of Babylon, captures Israelites and exile them to Babylon in the country called Assyria (formerly Sumer).

538 BC - Medo Persians conquered Babylon and allowed some of the Israelites to go back to their homeland and rebuild their temple that was destroyed by Babylon.

537 BC - Assyrians (Babylonians)   hire counselors (attorneys) against the Israelites to frustrate them in the building of the temple and weaken their hands (Ezra 4:5)

525 BC - Alexander the Great captures Babylon from the Medes and released the remnant of Israel back to their original homeland.

400 BC - Hebrew disappears as a language and the Israelites became scattered or "lost" by repeated captures and enslavement by Assyria - hence "the lost tribes of Israel." Many believe remnants of the Israelites tribes wandered to Northern Europe and carried the Biblical laws with them. Many also believe that America is the re-gathering of the lost tribes of Israel.

363 BC - Flavius Julianus (Julian the Apostate) begins reign as Emperor of Rome and soon seizes Babylon from Assyria adopting Babylonian Law (civil and maritime law) into Roman Law.

361 BC - Flavius Julianus greatly reduced taxes by cutting court expenditures and corruption. He was killed in battle with the Persians.

200 BC - Two Roman Emperors are assassinated for passing usury laws.

133 BC - Babylonian priests turn over priesthood to Roman priesthood in Pergamos in western Turkey, the future site of the Seven Churches in Revelation where Pergamos is referred to as "Satan's Seat" or throne.

Physical Babylon is destroyed but the system they established lingers, even to this day.

88 BC - Brutus assassinates Julius Caesar as Emperor for allowing Roman Government to mint coins and make money plentiful in strong opposition of private money-changers (banks and Babylon)

33 AD - Christ chases the money changers (banks) out of the temple and 3 days later is charged with blasphemy by Pharisees (lawyers) and is crucified.

The significance of the Bible and some of the events described therein is that all law is based upon the biblical prescriptions and prohibitions. It is important to note the reasons and rational behind the formation of these laws and how they have influenced society throughout the ages. From Moses to Jesus, the scribes wrote of upheavals based on famine, slavery, the desire for wealth, greed, and the control of populations by the elite few. it should also be noted that those in power or who had influence who refused to accept the dictates of controlled commerce were killed or overthrown. When decisions were made to benefit the masses as opposed to the select few, it was not long thereafter that the ruler or head of state who made that decision was eliminated.

Also of note is the end result of too much power and too much control being in the hands of a select few. Unable to continually enslave large and growing populations, eventually the people would rebel. There have been continual revolutions and wars based upon the rejection of economic and/or political enslavement. Usually after these shifts in power, things improve for the masses. Then, as history repeats itself, an elite group or powerful dictator gains control, becomes an imperialist, and enacts laws that restrict commerce for the benefit of the few. Then, the cycle starts anew.

Until the Eighth Century, AD, the Anglo-Saxons still practiced religious devotion with a lively appreciation. Their law was the Bible and it was most of the ancient Biblical principles which characterized the precepts of People's Law. It was a system designed to preserve and protect the unalienable rights of the people. At the same time, provided a divided, balanced, limited form of government.

As Thomas Jefferson, one of the authors of the Declaration of Independence discovered, the institutes of the Anglo-Saxons were almost identical with those of ancient Israel, which had the oldest system of representative government known to history.

American history is entrenched in and bound to the history of England. To understand the roots of our system, it is very important to know and recognize the historical events of England. To this day, our laws and systems of business, law and government are inextricably bound to our past with England and England's history. It is only through this contextual lens that we can see where we are heading and why.

RULER'S LAW

1000 AD - Goldsmiths (banks) took in gold as deposit and loaned out more receipts as loans than they had gold in reserve. This was the birth of the fractional reserve banking.

1100 AD - Henry I, took money power away from the money changers and established the tally stick system which lasted nearly 500 years.

In 1066 AD, the Normans, under William the Conqueror, subjugated the English people and established a royal dynasty, which still occupies the throne of England to this day. The Normans imposed on the English a system of Ruler's Law which destroyed the rights of the people, resulted in the confiscation of much of their land, and inflicted a system of cruel oppression on people that was virtually unendurable.

It is important to note that throughout Europe, the rulers were connected to the rulers of other nations through what was deemed, "royal blood-lines". In effect, all of the land, wealth and productivity of the entire continent was concentrated and controlled by a handful of individuals. Across the world, the same type of control over the masses was being exacted by powerful dynasties in Asia. In South America, powerful tribes controlled vast territories and accumulated gold and silver to enrich and honor a very select few. In the Mediterranean and North Africa, there were continuous wars and battles over territory and control of material wealth, again for the benefit of a select few. None of the wars or conflicts were fought for the benefit of the people, yet it was the people, the masses of society who fought the wars, suffered and paid for the conquests of the emperors, kings and chiefs who were in power.

Using a hypothetical, we can simplify the reason why the peasants and commoners who were under the control of the elite participated. We can also illuminate a way some came to power. Finally, we can demonstrate the reasons behind the perpetual need for expansion. At different points in history, a man would lead an army into battle with a neighboring nation. As often quoted, to the victor go the spoils of war, and a winning general (used in this context as a generic term for chieftain, leader, etc.), who already has the loyalty of his forces, captures the material wealth of another city-state or nation. With that wealth, he was able to pay his loyal commanders and soldiers a wage greater than what could be earned through farming or producing goods.

Having the wealth (capital) to pay for an army and in a position to grant authority to his most trusted lieutenants, a general would thus be able to secure control over larger and larger territories. Using the force of his army and relying on the loyalty of those he has rewarded with titles, power and wealth, this leader obtains dominion over the land, material goods and people of the land he has conquered. His authority was not nor would it ever be in the best interest of the people. Yet, they would conform out of fear.

Through forms of taxation and with the use or threat of force exacted by his underlings, this leader assumes the title of "King" and subjects the people who live in the region of his influence to whatever rule of law he dictates. Because his army is organized and armed well beyond the means of even a large group of peasants, there was no way to resist the demands of a self-proclaimed ruler or king. The number of smaller kingdoms throughout the course of history is countless. The number of middle and larger dynasties are well known: Egyptians, Assyrians, Greeks, Romans, Goths, Normans, Mongols, Tartars, Saxons, Moores, Spanish, English and Huns...and theirs histories all follow the same trajectory. They all eventually collapsed under their own weight, seeking out more power, more territory and more wealth -- that which was necessary to control what they had created.

It is only logical that since a given territory would only have a limited amount of resources and material goods to posses, this necessitated further expansion. In order to conquer other lands, more peasants would be recruited into the army, paid and given both a title and responsibility. If a large portion of the men are subscribed to the army and another portion committed to creating and supplying the army while many of the remaining men are tasked with governing the realm, who is left to produce the material needs of the people? This cycle would continue to the point where very few people were actually producing anything except for what would sustain the army. A nation drained of wealth and with multitudes of troops to pay, a king would have to continue to conquer other territories in order to maintain the ability to remain in power.

There were times of many "kings" many territories and many wars. The Royal Blood-Line was the result of several very successful kings, granting of titles and control to relatives, along with inter-family marriages to consolidate power and control of vast territories. What were the masses to do? Faced with either accepting the king or being killed or imprisoned for disloyalty, the commoner lived in fear and did whatever the imperialistic leaders dictated. And, the kings and emperors, in order to maintain power had to constantly increase the size of his own court (government). In order to pay for armies, police, tax collectors, governors and the support each office required drained more and more resources. The choices were few, either take more from the people who the kings sought to control, or go to war and take other people's resources.

Throughout history, it has always been the commoners who suffer so that the elite can prosper. Whatever form of government that has control, by its very nature, grows a stomach that can never be filled because the more governments seek to control, the more resources they need. In a world of limited, scare resources, the burden of these governing structure eventually overwhelms the societies they seek to control. It is a simple equation in that the more people needed to enforce the rule of law, the less productive a society becomes. Then, that society must either obtain the needed resources from other territories or create wealth out of thin air. That is where the merchants bankers and law makers do their best work.

That leads us to the first truth we must accept, which has been proven time and time again throughout history: All governments exist in order to perpetuate their own existence. No matter what politicians say, nor what founding documents propose, the laws and the leaders have one purpose; not to benefit the people but to control them in order to insure and secure their own existence.

Part of the system created in England in order to maintain control of the population was the noble class. These were the people and descendants of those whom the king or previous kings had favored. The nobility were the only ones allowed to hold the titles for land in the British Empire and they consisted of Barons, Counts, Earls and Dukes. They were the governors of territories, the ones responsible for tax collection and enforcing the King's law upon the commoners. They, in turn, passed on a portion of the wealth they collected to the king, serving as his loyal subject. Only the king or queen could grant titles. Also, the titles held by the men and woman of nobility were conveyed upon their heirs. Marriages in nobility was arranged in order to consolidate power or increase influence. In this way, control of the entire nation, all if its wealth and all of its material possessions, remained in the hands of a select few.

THE MAGNA CARTA

(Magna means large; Carta means charter, hence large charter)

Because King John was one of the most cruel and ruthless of the Norman Kings, the Barons united their forces and compelled him to sign the famous Magna Carta. This was done on a hill at Runymede, England and under the threat of beheading King John if he did not sign the paper. The date was June 15, 1215. The Magna Carta not only returned to the people many of the rights which the conquerors had stolen away; it also acknowledged that King John himself, as well as future kings, were subject to the law.

The Magna Carta not only referred to the Rights of the barons, but also made frequent reference to the Rights of English "freeman." The American Founders counted themselves freemen and invoked the Magna Carta as a covenant on the part of the King and his heirs that those rights would always be respected. This initial victory in the partial recovery of their rights became a major step in American history. Interestingly enough, the Magna Carta is one of the basis of our laws in the United States.

EVOLUTION OF PARLIAMENTARY POWER

"Parliament" means a group of people who believe themselves to be superior by their own authority, making law in comfort and seclusion, without recourse or responsibility, to control common people who they consider to be of inferior quality and worthy of little regard.

The foundations of parliamentary government began to develop around 1265. This government gradually evolved into a legislative voice purported to represent the desires of the people. It also provided a bargaining tool to regain some of the lost powers of the people and limit the tyrannical powers of the king. The Parliament regained the right to have no taxation without the approval of the people's representatives. They also established the principle that there would be no laws imposed on the people that had not been fully approved by the Parliament. Finally, the Parliament secured the right to impeach the arrogant and abusive officers of the king whenever it could be shown that they had violated the law in the exercise of their high office.

The rise of parliamentary power only came about because a group of individuals who, through titles and wealth, retained the power to confront a king. It is only because the king was impinging upon the wealth of the lower noble class that these changes were exacted from a despotic king. The history of the Magna Carta was not lost on the American Colonists. In order to obtain the right of self determination, drastic action must be taken.

However, when changes occur and self-determination sought (such as inalienable rights or freedom from tyranny or economic servitude), it is not long before a counter-reformation takes place. Those with the wealth, the power, the influence and the means have and will, always go to great lengths to regain control. The history of England's Parliament and Prime Minister, those who wrested control of the empire from the King, shows that there was still not enough power given to the people in order to limit the power of government.

PARLIAMENTARY SUPREMACY

1500 AD - Henry VII, relaxed usury laws which infuriated the money changers.

1600 AD - Queen Elizabeth I, controls money supply and issues own coin against the wishes of the money changers.

1650 AD - Oliver Cromwell, financed by the money changers, had King Charles killed, then plunged England into debt from wars and took over the city of London.

1688 AD - England is monetarily exhausted after 50 years of war with France and Holland. The private Bank of England (Babylon) is formed and secures itself with politicians and their laws to protect the bank and the debt of England. The tally sticks are attacked by the Bank of England and they replace it with their own money system which took away the power of the King to control money.

1698 AD - English debt rocketed from 1.25 million pounds to 16 million pounds within a few years.

During the reign of two German Kings over England, (George I and George II between 1714 and 1760) the Parliament was left on its own more than ever before. The government was run almost entirely by the King's Prime Minister, which meant that he and other members of Parliament serving in the Prime Minister's Cabinet could appoint all of the officials and have a relatively free hand in running the government. This brought England to the status of a limited monarchy with a parliament system of government that allowed the legislature to exercise practically unlimited power. Simply stated, the power and control of the government over the people passed from a very select few individuals to a larger, yet still just a handful of powerful people. Though intended to give a voice to the commoners, the reality was that the Parliament and Prime Minister acted to enrich and entrench themselves and those who they favored. At the behest and under the instruction of the money-changers (financiers and bankers), the English Empire continued to accumulate debt. Despite the massive size of the British Empire and the wealth they accumulated from distant lands, the majority of the citizens of England were poor. Life in London and other cities of Europe during these times has been well documented. The feelings and attitudes toward the commons, and the lack of understanding of their plight, can be summarized by the words of a famous queen. When told that the people on the streets were starving because they had no bread, she told her court, "Let them eat cake!"

The governing system in England never rose above the step of Parliamentary power, nor did its commonwealths, Canada, Australia, and the others, which eventually followed the same pattern. The powerful remained in power, at the expense of the common man. With the advent of commercial trans-Atlantic passage, many frustrated Europeans began the migration to "America" in order to find spiritual and social freedom.

It was only in America that Englishmen acquired the advantages of self-determination. America was an English colony. However, it was where the first opportunity for local or provincial assemblies were developed in modern history. America was where the people elected the delegates. The first inauguration in Virginia was as early as 1619. As the colonies gained in economic and political strength, they demanded the full recognition of their rights as Englishmen.

It was at this time that the colonies asserted their inalienable rights of self-government by issuing the Declaration of Independence to the King of England. The people of America then confederated together as the United States. Their form of government was a confederated republic, where the states remained supreme.

Prior to the Revolution, most commerce was done by barter and paper money printed by different states. However, all of it was based on the production of goods and services created by the people. This is an important fact to remember. Trade conducted on the barter system and currency backed by material goods was the backbone of the economic system. In America, after the Constitution was adopted, only gold and silver could be used as money in the United States. Unfortunately, since 1933, all money is based purely on debt and credit. There is nothing backing the money in use today and the paper currency in circulation has no intrinsic value. It is only "valuable" because people accept it as "legal tender". The rationale and destructive nature of these practices will be discussed later in this chapter.

Only because the elite in England considered the colonies a "frontier" was there a dearth of lawmakers, bankers and politicos bent upon subjecting the colonists to the ways of the old world. As the colonies became established, there was a transition from the "New World" being dependent on Europe to survive, to America exporting goods and no longer needing the support of England. It is also because of the financial strength and vast resources (agricultural and otherwise) of America that the greedy eyes of England eventually trained it's sights on these shores.

England was in trouble. Years of wars, massive debts, and fiscal policies that drained the Empire's resources had led the Parliament and king down the road of further imperialism. The tobacco from the Americas, the sugar from the Caribbean, the gold and diamonds from Africa, none of that was enough to meet the needs of the people, the Crown or the burgeoning bureaucracies they had created. It took more than a kings ransom to fund the armies who sought to control populations spanning the entire globe. For example, trading in humans, in the form of slavery, was not beneath them, nor was oppressing entire nations in order to steal the commercial resources.

The British were not alone in this exploitation and needed to subsidize their armies and growing navies. The Spanish destroyed entire cultures in South America, spreading disease and killing thousands upon thousands of people in order to bring the gold and silver back to Europe. The Dutch colonized Africa, claiming territories that belonged to the indigenous people. The French also claimed territories for themselves, colonizing areas in order to reap the benefits of whatever resources they could find. Many of the European wars fought during this period were based upon the desire to accumulate wealth.

America, by the Declaration Of Independence, declared war on England. However, most people do not realize that the primary reason for the war was not "taxation without representation," but the forced payment of taxes to the king in gold, not paper money. America was flourishing by using a form of "fiat money" based on their production -- not a gold based system that could be manipulated by the king. The king could not "control" the fiat money system in America and therefore passed a law requiring everyone to pay taxes in gold only. The king had most of the gold - and the colonies had very little (scarcity/value), eventually unemployment ensued - and eventually the embittered and resentful souls cried for war.

1748 AD - Amshel Bauer in Germany opens a goldsmith shop under the name of Red Shield.

RECENT TIME LINE OF RIGHTS

The American colonies gained independence by force of arms and asserted Rights for the entire world by the Treaty of Peace in Paris, France after the Revolution, by writing Articles of Confederation. Eventualy the the Articles of Confederation were replaced by a new system of People's Law under a written constitution.

THE ARTICLES OF CONFEDERATION AND STATE SUPREMACY

The Article of Confederation were adopted, providing for individual state "supremacy" and a committee of the states functioning as a National Congress.

CONSTITUTIONAL SUPREMACY

The American Founders established Republic based on a system of "Constitutional Law." To understand the depth and breadth of the Constitution, it is suggested that one read The Federalist Papers. Written contemporaneously as the Articles of the Constitution were debated and drafted, the discussions concerning the individual elements of the Constitution is quite revealing.

With seemingly the best intentions, America's Founding Fathers sought to prevent centralized power. A prime example is the use of three independent branches of government (executive, legislative and judicial) and two congressional bodies (the House of Representatives and the Senate). The authors of the Constitution were determined to prevent the control of government to pass into the hands of a select few. They abhorred the idea of a king, royalty and being subjected to the whims of a few, at the expense of the many.

A close reading of the Constitution reveals that every Article and every Amendment in the original Bill of Rights was meant to limit the power of government and provide protections to the people. Only in modern times (for example, abolition and allowing for an income tax) was the Constitution amended to expand the power of the government over the people. A prime example of how the Framers of the Constitution attempted make sure that no one person or group would usurp control of the nation is the Second Amendment, the right to bear arms. The original intent of the Founding Fathers was that the citizens of the United States could not be denied the right to bear arms for the purpose of arming a militia to overthrow a government that did not adhere to the constitution. Contrasting that with Europe were the armies had the weapons and the elite had control of the armies. The Founders surely realized that to maintain freedom from tyranny, a populace must have a way to fight for their rights. Allowing citizens to bear arms was meant to be a check on unlimited government power and control.

America did win the Revolutionary war with England. There was, however, a malfunction in the plans for America. Money powers were waiting at the gate from the beginning.

This nation was founded upon the notion of self-determination. As stated previously, it was the onerous taxes (with the requirement to be paid in gold) and price controls implemented by the English Crown that compelled a revolution in America. The founding documents of this nation and the debates establishing our government make it clear: what the people wanted was freedom. A cornerstone of freedom and self-determination is economic freedom. What was established by declaring independence and what is written in the Constitution was supposed to be the foundation of freedom including: the rule of law but with limitations on government power, controls on governmental influence on commerce, along with no interference of property rights and limitations on taxation. All of these elements were economic and established as the purported basis of a free market economy. That was the clear, unambiguous, intended goal of the founding documents of this nation.

Of paramount importance in discovering what went wrong is determining under what authority the states and federal government were created and established and understanding the foundations of our system of government. The authority for the American Constitution is derived from:

1. The Bible
2. The Magna Carta which King John signed in 1215.
3. The Petition of Rights granted by King Charles I in 1628.
4. The Habeas Corpus Rights granted by King Charles II in 1679.
5. The English Bill of Rights granted by William and Mary in 1689.
6. The Articles of Confederation.

These six documents became the basis and guidelines in creating our Constitution. It is important to know at this point that any constitution must have some prior reference to establish it. Based on this premise, any and every constitution thereafter must have an enabling clause. To this day, the individual states cannot enact a law that denies them a right guaranteed by the Constitution, nor can their constitutions afford protections that are less than those granted by the United States Constitution. From this point onward, no constitution may diminish, in any manner, those rights already established in the above six documents.

Next, the people of the various states created the individual state governments (from the territories of the original thirteen colonies) for the protection of their rights. They delegated certain authority from the people powers by and through the state constitutions, in order that the three branches of government could properly carry out the dictates outlined in the constitutions to protect our rights. The States then created the United States.

The American Constitution created a new structure of government that was established and intended to be on a much higher plane than either the parlimentary system or the confederation of states. It was a people's "Constitutional Republic," where a certain amount of power was delegated to the states and a certain amount was delegated to the federal government. The United States, by way of the Congress of the United States, has certain powers delegated and enumerated by the Constitution. So far as the several States who were parties to the Constitution are concerned, the United States may not excercise power not delegated by the Constitution. All power not delegated to the United States by the Constitution is reserved to the several states within their respective territorial borders or, in other words, to the people.

Despite the seemingly good intentions of America's Founding Fathers, something went drastically wrong. To understand the reason behind the failure of the Constitution to protect the people and their interests, it becomes necessary to research deeper into the basis and language of the Constitution.

The Constitution was pushed and supported by the bankers through their associates, for their own control over the United States of America. Had the Articles of Confederation been completed and adopted, instead of the Constitution, the bankers would have far less control than they achieved.

One of the powers granted in the Federal Constitution is to the Congress in Article 1, Section 8, Clause 16 and 17, which reads as follows:

16. To exercise exclusive legislation in all causes whatsoever, over such district (not exceeding ten mile square) as may, by cession of particular states, and the acceptance of Congress, become the seat of the government of the United States, and to exercise like authority over all places purchased, by the consent of the legislature of the state in which the same shall be, for the creation of forts, magazines, arsenals, dock-yards, and needful buildings:

17. To make all laws which shall be necessary and proper for carrying into execution the foregoing powers, and all the new powers vested by this Constitution in the government of the United States, or in any department or officer thereof.

Congress has absolute -- or what is described as plenary power. This is municipal, police power, and the like.

Where does Congress have such plenary power. Read again clauses 16 and 17 above. Only within the geographical area of the District of Columbia, and all forts, magazines, arsenals, dock-yards, and needful buildings within the several States.

THE CONSTITUTION IS BIFURCATED — SEPARATED IN TWO PARTS

The Constitution was bifurcated. Bifurcated is defined as separated or divided. We will call it bifurcated because it is the separation from the original jurisdiction as outlined in the Articles of Confederation. Article 1, Section 8, Clause 16 and 17 clearly set this out. What is important to note is that the United States Congress does have the right to make all laws regarding Washington D.C. and within the ten miles square and territories owned by the United States, etc. According to the plain language of the Constitution, that is the extent of their power and that was what was intended. This tiny scope of legislative powers is the only authority relating to people of various states.

Considering the distaste the Framers of the Constitution had for being governed from afar, how would they then allow for distant territories to be subjected to the rule of law from a centralized power? The Federal Government as designed by the Framers, was meant for some very specific purposes:

1. National Defense.
2. International Commerce.
3. Protection of the Rights of the People.

Anything else was beyond the scope of the Federal Government and left to the States, or the people. Contrast these founding ideals with the way government is today and the multitude of laws, rules, restrictions, programs and other "functions" they have monopolized. Consider the size of government and all they do in relation to what is enumerated in the Constitution as specific limits of their power.

Also, consider the attitude of the British prior to the Revolutionary

War. The Times of London quoted the following in regards to America's finances:

If this mischievous fiscal policy, which has its origins in North America, shall become endurrated down to a fixture, then that government will furnish its own money without cost. It will pay off debts and be without debt. It will have all the money necessary to carry on its commerce. It will become prosperous without precedent in the history of the world. The brains and the wealth of all the countries will go to North America. That country must be destroyed or it will destroy every Monarchy in the world.

THE FIRST NATIONAL BANK IN THE UNITED STATES

Within two years after winning the war for independence, one of the first acts of President Washington was to declare an emergency. William Morris, with the help of Alexander Hamilton, Secretary of Treasury, heavily promoted the First United States Bank (Bank of England, Babylon) to the legislation in order to create a private bank. In 1781, Congress chartered the First National Bank for a term of 20 years, to the same European bankers that were holding the debts before the war. The bankers loaned worthless, un-backed, non-secured printed money to each other to charter the first bank.

The act of creating a national bank was beyond the scope of the authority granted in the Constitution. It is true that the early years of the United States were marked by erratic, unstable markets. However, this created an opening for the Europeans who saw the value, wealth and opportunity to expand into the fledgling Nation. The bankers and money-changes asserted their influence by introducing foreign currency into the American system. Also, they brought with them the practices and procedures common in Europe such as credit lending and charging onerous interest rates. Lending to the new American Government created the destabilization necessary to become entrenched in the American political scene.

There was little central planning in America and currencies from many nations corrupted the system of barter and trade. In 1790, on the advice of the Secretary of Treasury, Alexander Hamilton, Congress created the First United States Bank. The public believed this was done in order to eliminate inefficiencies in the young Republic by creating a standard currency. Also, that it was a place where the government could deposit its funds. The public was told that a national bank would help in the collection of taxes and assist both the government and businesses by increasing the amount of capital necessary for expansion. History is very kind and respectful to the Founding Fathers of the United States. It is unfortunate that such reverence tends to conceal the true events of history. Take for example, Benjamin Franklin. His place in history is seemingly well-settled in his brilliance as an inventor, writer, and negotiator. What is not known is that during the Revolutionary War, at his behest, the struggling nation systematically printed money while falsely claiming the fledging government had the reserves in gold to back it up. This very first "intervention" into the monetary system had catastrophic results as inflation rose to the point that the soldiers being paid with the worthless script found the paper currency more valuable to use as toilet paper. Franklin's actions were at the behest of French bankers, who were unwilling to fund the war against the British at the levels requested and required by the Americans. Those in power did not learn the costly lesson they should have when their attempt to float dollars backed by nothing backfired. After the Revolutionary War, the lawmakers in Philadelphia and then Washington D.C., continued to subscribe to deficit spending, borrowing money to pay for the expenses of the Nation. In order to do so, they had no choice but to act beyond the scope of the Constitution.

While it is true that the British Government lost the war in 1783, the East India Company's owners who constituted a portion of the invisible, (sovereign) Power structure (banks) behind the British Government did not lose. Instead, they moved right into the new American economy. Together, and in close association with America's most powerful land owners, the merchants, bankers and lawyers sank their hooks into the lifeblood of America, commerce.

At that time in our history, there were many "local" currencies and the power-brokers who sought to control the Nation had no control and no way to establish exchange rates. Although the local currencies were backed by product; the bankers, lawyers and politicians argued the system had the effect of destabilizing the Nation. Not having a national currency, they said, was inefficient and inadequate. The Federal Government had not established but argued for, and desired, a central planning agency to control the money supply.

As the bankers and money-changes asserted their influence by introducing foreign currency into the American system, they also brought with them the practices and procedures common in Europe, such as credit lending and charging onerous interest rates. Most significantly, they arranged for financing of the operation of the United States Federal Government through the private banks of Europe and the English Crown.

There was little to no central planning in Washington D.C. to protect the States from foreign influences. Currencies from many nations corrupted the system of barter and trade. As mentioned previously, in 1790, on the advice of the Secretary of Treasury, Alexander Hamilton, when Congress created the First United States Bank, the Nation was told that this was was done in order to eliminate inefficiencies in the young Republic by creating a standard currency. Also, it was a place where the government could deposit its funds. The public was told that a national bank was necessary to assist in the collection of taxes and assist both the government and businesses by increasing the amount of capital necessary for expansion. What the public was not told was what was pledged as collateral for the loans. The funds that were borrowed had to be collateralized and, once again, acting beyond the powers granted to them by the Constitution, Congress pledged the future productivity of all Americans in order to secure the loans.

The First United States Bank's charter was granted in 1791, but expired 20 years later in 1811. After years of dissension from rural and Southern States, the Senate refused to grant a new charter. Creating the First United States Bank had one clear result, it empowered the merchants, money-changers and lawyers in the cities, while harming the farmers and producers of goods in the rural communities. After only twenty years of playing by the rules of the old-world, the system had become totally corrupt.

Having an agriculture based economy, the farmers were subject to season cycles and, at times, poor crop yields from bad weather. In order to buy seed for the following year's crop, the farmer could not pledge part of the crop yield in exchange for the seed. The merchants and bankers would send the farmer to the bankers who would force the farmer to use his land as collateral. That way, if the crop failed again, the bank would recover their investment in property. For the "privilege" of putting a lien on the farmer's property and loaning him the money to buy the seed, the bankers tacked on a large interest rate, one that they knew the farmer could only repay under the best of circumstances. The farmer would plant his seed and pray. The merchant would take the money and deposit it back into the bank so that the bankers could loan the SAME MONEY to other farmers.

If there was a bumper crop, the farmers would go to the merchants to sell their goods. Since there was so much supply, the merchants would refuse to pay fair prices, leaving the farmers with unsold good and little money. Then, when the many farms could not keep up with even the interest payments, the lawyers would come in and file the paperwork needed to seize their farms. Either way, good seasons or bad, the bankers and lawers always won.

This vicious cycle was repeated so often over the past 200-years, that 90% of all farmland is now owned by a small handful of international corporations. To no one's surprise, sitting on the board of directors as majority shareholders of these major corporations are the same several families who own and control the twelve Federal Reserve Banks. Also, this cycle was imposed horizontally into almost every single industry in the Country. This is part of what gave rise to the "Robber Barons" and the control of the vast majority of the Nation's wealth by a select few. You must ask yourself, was this what the Framer's intended?

This chain of events was not new to history, only a different more subtle method was used to usurp almost all of the wealth and property of this Nation. Instead of vast armies conquering the territories, the bankers and lawyers created a system where after they collected their profits, in the end they would get the land as well. Commoners holding the title to property was an anathema to the nobility. What is different today? How many people actually own the homes they live in? Very few because the banks own them (through mortgages). The states own them (through tax liens). And the so-called "American Dream" is nothing but an illusion.

None of this would have happened or have even been possible if the leaders in Washington D.C. followed the Supreme Rule of Law, the Constitution. By exceeding their bounds and establishing the means for the merchants, bankers and lawyers to operate, the political class succeeded in expanding their own personal power, control and wealth. Again, this was done at the expense of the people as a whole.

At the same time the Fist United States Bank was chartered, protectionist policies, first advocated by Hamilton and initiated in 1791, imposed tariffs on foreign goods. This was supposedly done in order to allowed newly formed industries in the United States to grow. Again in 1816, large tariffs were levied against European goods as the British sold low-cost merchandise into the American market. The leaders of our nation felt that this was an attempt to squeeze American manufacturers out of business. The government intervention into the free-market economy was a disaster with levies and taxes that inhibited and hindered commerce.

There are always unintended consequences when commerce is restricted and the government's tariffs intended to protect specific industries harmed more people than it helped. The British simply passed on the expense of the levies to the American consumers. When lawmakers act, extending their power and control over commerce, restricting trade, setting price controls, they are doing exactly what the British did which caused the colonists to revolt. It was the government who collected the taxes and levies. It was the government extending its reach and power and control over the people, not to help to people, but to insinuate themselves in the middle of commerce. Trade and economic activity was actually hindered by the same people who purported to act for the benefit of the people. From that time forward, there has never been a period of "free commerce." The political class, in order to sustain itself, would always get their cut!

After thousands of lives were lost fighting a war to get control of our own money, why did Congress contract with the same bankers that started the revolutionary war in the first place? Very simple. Since the Crown (Rothchild) was the creditor, they demanded a private bank to hold the securities of the United States as the pledged assets to the Crown of England in order to secure the debt to which the United States had defaulted. The holder of the securities was the private bank. So under Public International Law, the creditor nation forced the United States to establish a private bank to hold the securities as the collateral for the loan. As has happened throughout history, Babylon follows wherever we go. So, the question remains, who was behind the corruption of the American system?

EUROPEAN BANKERS EXPAND

1785 AD - The youngest Rothchild, Nathan, expanded his wealth to 20,000 pounds in 15 year period by using other peoples money. An increase of 2500%.

1787 AD - Amshel Rothschild made the famous statement: "Let me issue and control a nation's money, and I care not who writes the laws."

24

Thomas Jefferson stated, "If the American People ever allow the previous banks to control the issue of their currency, first by inflation and then by deflation, the banks and the corporations which grow up around them will deprive the people of all property until their children wake homeless on the continent their fathers conquered."

1798 AD - The five Rothschild brothers expanded by opening banks in each of the major cities of Europe. Amshel Mayer, Germany; Solomon, Vienna; Jacob, Paris; Nathan, London; Carl, Naples.

THE WAR OF 1812 AND THE SECOND NATIONAL BANK

The charter for the private bank called The First National Bank was for 20 years — until around 1811. What happened in 1812? The War of 1812. What did England attack? Washington, D.C. The ten miles square where they burned the White House and other buildings.

Was the attack by England on the ten square miles an act of war on their part? No, it was not. It was an act of retaliation and a "shot across the bow". The British burned Washington because the United States failed to meet its obligations under the debt agreements signed between the United States and the bankers of England. By failing to renew the charter of the First National Bank, the U.S. violated collateral requirements which were a covenant of the American debt held by the British. Under public international law, what it was seemingly an act of war by England was actually a result of America's "act of war" -- failing to meet its international obligations.

When the United States did not extend the First United States Bank into the Second National Bank to continue to maintain the securities on an unpaid debt, the United State was in fact in default. So what the United States did was, as defined by international law was an act of war -- not giving the lawful creditor his securities in a peaceful manner. The only remedy open under international law to the creditor was to come in on "letters of marquee" and seize assets to protect his loan. Please note that the Bank of England used the authority of the Sovereign, the British Empire, to collect their debts. That fact leaves little doubt about who controls whom.

Did the national bank get approved? Absolutely. After England attacked the Nation that was in default, the American political class saw the light and enacted the Second United States Bank. It was either that, or watch as every city in North America was sacked, the riches stolen and the Nation destroyed. The Charter for the Second National Bank was for another 20 years.

During the War of 1812, altough it was stated that in order to finance the war, the Government was forced to sell bonds, bills and notes and institute direct taxes; the fact of the matter is **that** the United States Federal Government needed to capitialize (i.e. establish the collateral necessary) in order to secure the debt they owed to the Rothschild. Because of that experience, Congress chartered the Second Bank of the United States in order to hold the reserves and accumulate more, as required by the terms of the debt.

In selling the concept of a national bank to the public, it was argued that "the prosperity of the people" was dependent on the stability and reliability of the currency as a means of trade. After another two decades had passed, and caught between the desire to limit the influence of the Federal Government and the need for a stable banking system, our political leaders, wisely and bravely chose a "hands-off" approach to banking. In 1836, the Charter of the Second United States Bank expired. However, like all brave men who act upon the interest of the people, the man with the conviction to stand behind the law of the land, our Constitution, was impeached.

THE ORIGINAL 13TH AMENDMENT

There was another important issue involved in the War of 1812. The original 13th Amendment, which expressly prohibited attorneys or anyone with a title of nobility, to hold any public office in America. All the states then ratified this 13th Amendment, with the exception of Virginia.

You'll note that the War of 1812 was waged mostly in Washington, D.C. That was by design since the invading forces had several very specific goals. The British burned all the repository buildings and attempted to destroy all records of the new United States in Washington, D.C. Because the British were aware of a fundamental shift in not only the public attitude, but also the political will of America's elected officials, part of their strategy was to hide the true nature of their involvement in the foundation of America. To eradicate the evidence of their involvement and those behind the changes that allowed for the accumulation of debt to England, they sought to destroy the evidence.

Another reason why the War of 1812 was waged was to prevent

the passage and enforcement of the new 13th Amendment. Most book repositories through the States were burned to the ground and all records destroyed. There is a famous painting in Washington, D.C. (and it can be found in many books) depicting the British boarding a ship after they "surrendered." The painting showed the British carrying their rifles as they mounted the gangplank. One must ask, "What army is allowed to keep their weapons after they surrender?" One must also ask, "Who really won the war?"

ANDREW JACKSON AND THE BANK.

President Andrew Jackson put an end to this second charter in 1836. Jackson's reasoning was simple: The Constitution does not delegate authority for Congress to establish a national Bank. Jackson's rationale has never been seriously challenged and the Constitution has never been amended to authorize Congress to establish a national bank. Nor, for that matter, does the Constitution delegate authority for the United States to establish corporations, particulary private corporations.

There was not a national bank established in America for more **than** 75 years, until 1913, with the Federal Reserve Bank. Without question, Andrew Jackson did an excellent job.

What did Congress do with Andrew Jackson? They impeached him. Because Congress is made up of mostly attorneys, who hold the title of "Esquire", one must ask themselves, to whom did the attorneys owe their title of nobility to? The Crown of England. So, since Congress is populated by attorneys who are Esquires (retaining titles of nobility to the Crown of England), the question thus becomes, who exactly does our Congress represent? The Bankers.

It was the bankers who hired an assassin to kill Andrew Jackson using two pistols, however the plot failed as both pistols misfired. Just like other famous leaders of the past who tried to protect the masses, Jackson's life was at risk. Andrew Jackson was to be killed because he violated public international law when he denied the creditor their just lien rights on the debtor. However, in Jackson's mind, and in reality, the bankers did not lend value (substance), so in actuality they had an unperfected lien. Under that scenario, the law actually did not apply and Andrew Jackson **was** in the right.

THE CIVIL WAR

In 1860-61, the Southern States walked out of Congress. This created sine die. Abraham Lincoln was elected President. The South seceded and declared their state's rights pursuant to the Constitution. Despite the common understanding behind the impetus of the Civil War, slavery was only window dressing. The war had nothing to do with slavery. Instead, the war was fought over state's rights and the national debt to the bankers. The South wanted to be redeemed from the Crown of England. The North wanted to remain under their dominion and their debt.

When the South walked out of Congress, this ended the public side of the bifurcated Constitution as far as the government was concerned. What remained of the government was the private side, the democracy under the rule of the bankers.

During and after The Civil War, the new 13th Amendment was enacted December 18, 1865; the 14th Amendment was enacted July 28, 1868; the 15th Amendment was enacted March 30, 1870.

President Lincoln, by Executive Order, proclaimed the first Trading With The Enemy Act.

President Lincoln stated, "The government should create, issue, and circulate all currency and credit needed to satisfy the spending power of the government and the buying power of consumers." Further, he quoted, "The privilege of creating and issuing money is not only the supreme prerogative of government, but it is the governments' greatest opportunity."

It was not much longer afterwards that he was murdered. What history does not tell you is that President Lincoln was murdered because he defied the bankers by printing interest free money to pay for the war effort.

The 14th Amendment brought the freed slaves, whose previous owners were private plantation owners and transferred those slaves under slavery of the government, the ten miles square jurisdiction of Washington, D.C.

At this period of time, the only people in the United States who were under the jurisdiction of the private bifurcated government of the ten miles square of Washington, D.C, were the government employees, those who were within the territories owned by the United States and now, the former slaves. The former citizens of the South, now "captured" became the 14th Amendment citizens. The remainder of the people could still invoke the power over government through original jurisdiction of the Republic side of the Constitution. Thus, the government operated fully under the authority of private law dictated by the creditor.

In 1871 the default again loomed and bankruptcy was eminent. So in 1871, the ten square miles was incorporated in England. They used the Constitution as their own bylaws. Not as authority under the Constitution, but as authority over the Constitution. They copyrighted, not only the Constitution, but also many names including their own. This is the final blow to the original constitution. From here on out, the United States was governed by corporate law, dictated by the banks as creditors.

In the year 1913, under the leadership of President Woodrow Wilson, the Federal Reserve Act was passed. The creation of a central bank was a major step away from a "pure" free-market economy and the most notable public display of the entrenchment of the banking class. There was no longer any question, the Federal Government commanded control over the economy and the major factors that control economic conditions.

Prior to the enactment of the Federal Reserve Act, Federal action was taken to even the playing field and to reduce the power and influence of several monopolies in specific industries. Contrary to a pure capitalistic system, intervention through the Interstate Commerce Act (1887), The Sherman Anti-Trust Act of 1890 and the Clayton Act of 1914 empowered the Federal Government to break monopolies that had an adverse effect on the economy and consumers. Using these powers, the result was intended to increased competition and reduced prices. However, behind the scenes, enough loopholes were created so that the wealth and power behind the monopolies were retained while the public (the masses) were appeased.

When Standard Oil was broken up, the same families controlled the majority of the shares in the remaining daughter companies. To this day, of the Fortune 500 companies, the boards of directors and majority shareholders are all populated by the same names or relatives of the same people who controlled the wealth of this Nation in the late 1800's. Also, on the same boards are relatives or people connected to the owners of the Twelve Federal Reserve Banks, all private banks that make up the Federal Reserve System. This is public information that can be seen through SEC filings of each corporation's 10-K reports. It is a spiderweb of connectivity which proves that 80-90% of this Nation's wealth belongs to less than 2% of the population and is controlled by a small handful of families. The lineage of these families contains the offspring of the Vanderbilts, Rockefellers, Mellons, Carnegies and, of course, the Rothschilds.

How did the control of the Nation's wealth pass to the banking class? Because the political class (layers) enabled and allowed it to happen. Congress, again acting beyond their authority, gave control of the Nation's money supply to private individuals. Having one currency, creating markets for commercial paper (short-term loans) and the ability to manipulate the amount of currency in circulation, gave the Federal Reserve System the ability to control business cycles, businesses and the people. The creation of the Federal Deposit Insurance Corporation (FDIC) in 1935, was intended to give Americans confidence in the banking system, that their savings were in fact safe. Using the tools of interest rate manipulation and bond purchases or sales, the Government had in place what it needed to maintain control of the American economy. These was no longer free trade and commerce was adversely affected.

MORE BANKRUPTCY RE-ORGANIZATIONS

In 1909, America's potential default loomed once more. The U.S. Government went to the Crown of England and asked for an extension of time. This extension was granted for another 20 years on several conditions. One of the conditions was that the United States allow creditors to establish a new national bank. This was done in 1913, with the Federal Reserve Bank. This, along with the 16th Amendment, collection of Income Tax, enacted February 25, 1913, and the 17th Amendment enacted May 31, 1913, were conditions for the extension of time. The 16th and 17th Amendments further reduced the States power. The United States had fully adopted the Babylonian system.

THE FIRST WORLD WAR

In 1917, the United States was drawn into the First World War. The debt accumulated to such a vast sum that it became impossible for the nation to pay off when the debt came due in 1929. The government, in order to try and solve the problem, enhanced the War Powers Act that President Lincoln, by Executive Order put in place during his Presidency. This War Powers Act was re-enforced as was the Trading with the Enemy Act of 1917, This will become more important later on.

THE GREAT DEPRESSION

We all know what happened in 1929. This was the year of the stock market crash and the beginning of The Great Depression.

The Great Depression: The stock market crash moved billions of dollars from the people to the banks. This also removed cash from circulation for the peoples' use. Those who still possessed any cash, invested in high yielding Treasury Bonds. the value of the bonds were thus driven higher by increased demand. As a result, even more cash was removed from circulation for the general public, to the point where there was not enough cash left in circulation to buy the goods being produced. Production came to a halt as inventory overcrowded the market. There were more products on the market than there was cash to buy them. Prices plummeted and industries plunged into bankruptcy, throwing millions more people out of work and out of cash. Foreclosures on homes, factories, businesses and farms rose to the highest level in the history of America. A mere dime, was literally the salvation to many families who were living on the street. Millions of people lost everything they had, keeping only the clothes on their backs.

"The difficult questions concerning paper [money] are not about its economy, convenience or ready circulation but about the amount of paper that can be widely issued or created, and the possibilities of violent convulsions when it gets beyond bounds."

F. W. Taussig, Principles of Economics, 4th Ed., 1946.

John Maynard Keynes was an English economist who developed theories as to why the economies of many nations had collapsed. Based on his work, an entire school of thought was developed and policies enacted based on his theories. Keynsian Economics, is based on the premise that capitalism does not have self-regulating mechanisms and cannot be relied upon to run itself.

During the Depression, Keynsian thought played a major role in determining a course of action in order to stabilize the economy. Governmental fiscal actions, it was determined, can have an important stabilizing effect. After World War II, when it seemed as if the same problems encountered during the Great Depression were developing, Congress passed the Employment Act of 1946. In that act, they set forth the groundwork wherein the Federal Government was empowered to take actions through fiscal and monetary policy in order to maintain economic stability. With the fear of another depression looming, the public did not argue or fight what would be the final nail in the coffin of economic freedom. With the passage of these acts and the public acceptance, the United States Federal Government gained full control of all commerce.

One of the tools used was discretionary fiscal policy. That is the deliberate manipulation of taxes and government spending by Congress to offset cyclical fluctuations in output and employment. Free trade and unrestricted commerce were things of the past.

The process of taxation and spending by the government can be extremely complicated. The effects are delayed and have ramifications beyond the obvious. There are many variables such as deficit spending and the method by which public spending is financed. There is no question that fiscal policy can and does have a direct impact on the economy as a whole. For every law or tax or regulation created, there is a requirement of more people needed to check, account for and make sure the laws and regulations are followed. By enacting laws and creating these Byzantine regulations, the government must increase in size and complexity in order to maintain control. And, what is used to pay for these new government employees? The taxes and fees that were just imposed by the government itself.

What is the difference between the armies of the Dark Ages and Middle Ages and the governments of today? They were armed with swords to take the king's taxes. The government today has a police state behind them with prosecutors and black robed judges to fine you, take your property and throw you in jail. It is all about government control of all commerce.

What is the result of over-regulation and government control? Think of the percentage of American workers who work for the government (federal, state and local) and think of what they produce for their pay. The vast majority of them are employed to ensure that we the people follow their rule of law. Now, add in the lawyers, bankers, insurance agents, financial consultants, marketers and accountants along with the other "professionals" in service industries. What is the net product of their work? They produce nothing, yet are the highest paid members of our society.

So, how does the government pay for these millions and millions of employees? Either through higher taxes or by borrowing more money. One of the biggest debates after the level of taxation is about when the government creates money to pay its bills or fund projects. These questions are where Keynesian economists and monetarists clash.

"Monetarists" are economists who believe that government regulation, taxation and redistribution of income has created the system that has harmed the American people. Though they seem to be pointing to the truth, one must be careful. More than most, the monetarists side with the bankers and their arguments have subtle, hidden undertones that side with the ideals of the merchants, money-changers and lawyers. Their goal is ultimately to make the rich richer and keep the commoners in their place.

The practices of these theorists were put into place by Ronald Reagan. His policy was that if they cut the taxes and regulations of the very rich, the masses would prosper as the wealth "trickled down" through the economy. It is important to note that in the many years since, the "trickle down" theory of economics has not worked. As reported by many sources, real wages for laborers has not increased. The very wealthy now control a greater percentage of the world's assets than ever before. George Bush continued these policies, then following what was called, "supply-side economics." The Bush tax cuts enacted from 2000 to 2008 had the effect of concentrating wealth even more.

The disparity between the super-wealthy (the top 2% of earners) and the middle class has never been greater. In addition, the deregulation of the financial industry resulted in the catastrophic failure of industry titans, which required massive capital injections to keep banks solvent. After George Bush's supply-side economic policies, the United States was on the brink of another Great Depression. Supply-side economics, despite the poor track record (massive national debt, housing bubble, credit crunch, financial collapse, more Americans living below the poverty line, stagnant real wage growth) has contributed to economic to the bottom lines of the bankers and the very wealthy, at the expense of everyone else. We have to ask ourselves, was this a mistake or by design?

THE POWERS OF THE FEDERAL RESERVE

With the creation of the Federal Reserve, the Board of Governors has the responsibility of controlling the operation of our monetary and banking systems. This is the stated objective of the Federal Reserve: "The fundamental objective of monetary policy is to assist the economy in achieving a full-employment and a non-inflationary level of total output." Basically, monetary policy concerns altering the nation's money supply.

Loosening and tightening of the availability of money has been the method the Federal Reserve has used to influence the economy. Setting target interest rates has been their primary tool. When banks deposit funds with the Fed, the Fed pays them interest. This is a recent development because in the past, the Fed did not pay interest on reserves. In addition, the Fed sets a target rate that banks pay to each other for short-term loans. By lowering the interest rate, there is less of an incentive (less profit potential for banks) to deposit funds into the Federal Reserve or to loan money to another bank. Banks then have the profit incentive to loan money to the people. What interest rates banks charge consumers has a direct correlation to the Federal Reserve's manipulation of the rates they pay and the target rates they set.

For borrowers, lower interest rates and more money available makes it easier to get loans and it costs them less. Thus, maintaining low target rates is termed a "loose" monetary policy, because loans are cheaper and easier to obtain. The availability of credit at low rates increases the demand for goods and services.

Conversely, the Federal Reserve can raise the interest rates they pay banks, and the rates banks can charge each other. The effect of more money being put into reserve, where the banks earn a guaranteed rate of return, decreases the amount of money being loaned. The less money there is to loan, the harder it is to get a loan, and the more expensive it is to borrow money. This results in less economic activity. Raising interest rates is called "tightening", because it is harder to get loans.

In addition to manipulating interest rates, the Federal Reserve can also increase or decrease the percentage of deposits member banks are required to hold in reserve. This function enables the Federal Reserve to manipulate the overall money supply.

Another tool at the Federal Reserve's disposal in order to tighten or loosen the money supply is the buying and selling of Treasury bills, bonds and notes. The Federal Government, through the United States Treasury, borrows money and the Federal Reserve buys some of the debt instruments (loans the money) and holds the securities. In times of inflation, to reduce the amount of money in the money supply, the Federal Reserve can sell the Treasury bonds it holds to the public (individuals, firms, and foreign governments) . The money they take in from the sale of the bonds has the effect of reducing the amount of money in the economy. At other times, the Fed does the opposite — they buy bonds from the public, paying out cash and increasing the money supply.

Policies based upon the Keynsian theories, and in use since the 1940's, are quite diverse. Through the Federal Reserve's Board of Governors, certain control techniques are used to influence the size of member bank's reserves. Because excess reserves are what is used to expand the money supply through lending, any manipulation of excess reserves has a direct impact on the money supply. This is a function of the amounts commercial banks can and are willing to lend at certain interest rates. Interest rates are determined by the supply of money. Changes in the supply of money will effect interest rates and the amount of credit bankers are willing to make available to borrowers.

Just like in the days of the past, what the Federal Reserve promotes is fractional reserve lending. The member commercial banks are only required to keep a small percentage of the people's deposits on hand. The rest they loan out. When the money they loan out comes back into the banking system (say, as a seller's deposit), the bank puts only a fraction of that in reserve and loans it out a second time. They do it over and over in what is called, "the money multiplier". This is how money is created out of thin air.

It was theorized that changes in the cost and availability of loans has a direct impact on the spending habits of society. It also has an impact on the investment decisions of individuals and businesses. That, in turn, has an impact on the level of output, employment, income, and prices. We have seen this in effect since this country has fallen into a deep recession in late 2008. The Federal Reserve has kept interest rates as low as possible in order to try and increase production, reduce unemployment and get the economy stable. Along with massive spending by Congress (fiscal policy) it begs the question, what exactly is meant by "stable"?

The Federal government should not have intervened. The competitive marketplace would have, in fact, automatically allocate resources efficiently enough to correct the imbalances of 2008. The intervention into the banking system was clearly the biggest economic policy blunder ever made. Of course, that is viewing it from the standpoint of the common citizen. Governmental decision making is fraught with bureaucratic inefficiencies that are harmful to individuals. We can frequently point to policy mistakes and that centralized government control eventually leads to the loss of individual freedom. (Milton Friedman, Capitalism and Freedom, Chicago: The University of Chicago Press, 1962.) Instead, viewing from the banker's perspective, it was the quickest, easiest, largest transfer of wealth in the history of man. The same banks that were bailed out in 2008 have since paid out the largest bonuses ever recorded in January of 2010! To the bankers, the bailout by the Federal Government was their duty, or maybe better stated, a debt obligation.

The fact is, the economy would provide stability and full employment if it were not for the intervention and interference of the government. For example, wage-price flexibility would work if the government did not set a minimum wage, did not advance pro-union legislation or provide price supports for agricultural goods. The government creates rigidities which weaken the ability of market forces to provide stability. The tools used by government aggravate the instability they are meant to fix. By saving the major banks and insurance companies, the Federal Government only perpetuated a corrupt system.

Also, imagine the level of production that could be achieved if the non-producing members of our society actually produced something. Instead, on average, they are higher paid than private-sector workers, have better benefits and retire sooner than the average worker. The irony is that they (government employees) are living on taxes the government has imposed on the people and their job is to subjugate the people. It is the government growing in order to perpetuate itself. Make no mistake about it, this is all by design. To whom are the politicians beholden to? To what ends do they keep the citizens in perpetual debt?

The result of their manipulation has finally been revealed. In 2008 and 2009, the Federal Reserve Bank, by proxy, became the largest land-owner in the world. On their balance sheets they retain the rights to trillions of dollars worth of collateralized mortgage bonds. These were bought from commercial banks for pennies on the dollar and is the largest transfer of wealth in history. Approximately seven out of ten homeowners who have mortgages either owe money to the Federal Reserve (indirectly), to Fannie Mae or Freddie Mac (the two government financed mortgage lenders). Who owns everything? The bankers . . . the heirs and cronies of the same families who manipulated our currency in the first order more than 200 years ago.

To understand the forces at work, again, we look to history and attempt to make sense of the interplay between nations and the bankers. What effect did the debt the Federal Government owed at the founding of this Nation play on the world stage in later years? More importantly, we, the freemen of this Nation, how did we let this happen?

In Europe, in 1930, the International Bankers declared several nations bankrupt, including the United States. Then in 1933, President Roosevelt was elected into office. His first act as President was to declare, publicly, the United States bankrupt. He further went on to issue his Presidential Executive Order on March 5, 1933 that all United States Citizens must turn in all their gold in return for Federal Reserve Notes. This was passed into law by Congress on June 5th, 1933.

To understand the forces at work, again, we look to history and attempt to make sense of the interplay between nations and the bankers. What effect did the debt the Federal Government owed at the founding of this Nation play on the world stage in later years? More importantly, we, the freemen of this Nation, how and why did we let this happen?

In Europe, in 1930, the International Bankers declared several nations bankrupt, including the United States. Then in 1933, President Roosevelt was elected into office. His first act as President was to publicly declare the United States bankrupt. He further went on to issue his Presidential Executive Order on March 5, 1933 that all United States Citizens must turn in all of their gold in return for Federal Reserve Notes. This was passed into Law by Congress on June 5th, 1933.

We the people, turned in all our gold at that time. Why? Were we United States Citizens? No. We were still a sovereign people until that time. We just thought that we were required to turn in all our gold. Only those people living in Washington D.C. and the 14th Amendment Citizens were so required. We were still sovereign. We were not under the jurisdiction of the United States of America, which was incorporated in 1871.

At that time, the people of America were being manipulated. It is a known, documented fact that the price of gold (what the government would exchange in Federal Reserve Notes) was set by Roosevelt himself. Based on nothing but manipulation, he would change the going rate of exchange so that on days or weeks he would set the price higher, more people would turn in their private stocks of gold. Then, he would lower the price drastically, setting up the next rally -- and people sought to exchange their gold before the price dropped again. It was a ploy that worked.

When we turned in our gold, we unknowingly volunteered into the jurisdiction of the ten square miles of Washington, D.C. and their laws. We became 14th Amendment Citizens. Our Birth Certificates, the title to our bodies, all of our property and all of our future labor, was pledged to the International Bankers as security for the money owed in bankruptcy.

This was done under the authority of commercial law, (Babylonian Law) by and through Title. The American people were not in bankruptcy. Only the Corporate United States was in bankruptcy. Yet, the Federal Government usurped us to cover the debts they themselves had incurred. When sovereign Americans turned over their gold, they also turned over their freedom and rights of self-determination.

Again, we must remember that it was only the politicians and the ten miles square of Washington, D.C. the United States Corporation that went into bankruptcy. It was not the American people. To fully understand this, is important to remember the exact language of the Constitution and the provisions concerning the powers of the legislative branch. Congress was not acting on behalf of the American people, because they had no constitutional authority to do so,

Neither did the President, through Executive Order, have the power to accumulate debt, forcibly remove gold from circulation nor replace the gold (and silver certificates) with Federal Reserve Notes. These acts were, therefore illegitimate. Through the manipulation of their money, they now control us all.

WHAT IS MONEY?

There are various functions of money. Primarily, money is a means of exchange that can be used in buying and selling goods and services. Money is also a standard of value, what society uses as a "measuring stick" to determine the relative worth of various goods and services. Stating prices using one common standard allows consumers to compare the relative worth of many commodities.

Finally, money serves as a store of value, because it is the most liquid of all assets, i.e., it can be directly exchanged for goods and services. Other assets such as commodities, must be sold first, or used in barter.

Because of the many uses of money, there is demand for it. People need money as a medium of exchange, or transactional demand. Money allows people and businesses to conduct transactions to meet their needs. The larger the amount of all goods and services exchanged in the economy, the more money needed to negotiate these transactions.

The second factor that creates demand for money is asset demand. People hold their assets and seek to retain the value of those assets in various forms. Beyond the actual currency itself, money is used to procure all other asset classes. There can be a cost associated with holding money if interest rates are high and people who are adverse to seeing the value of their money decline, seek to invest it in asset classes that have rising values.

Our currency is "fiat money" in that it has no intrinsic value. In other words, there in nothing at all to support its value. Instead it is backed ONLY by the full faith and credit of the United States Government.

Currency is a debt of our government, whereas demand deposits are a debt to banks. The thought that the currency we deal with has any worth is only an illusion and the illusion only works because the next person believes in it as well. But, logically speaking, if you are paid in dollars (Federal Reserve Notes) what is being passed to you is a debt obligation of the United States Government. The U.S. Government is itself insolvent and when you consider that repayment of outstanding Treasury Bills, Bonds and Notes, the statement that money is NOT worth the paper it is printed on in absolutely true. The Federal Reserve is under no obligation to repay the loan (notes) with anything of material value. In effect, dollars are only worth something because people believe it is. It is a complete delusion.

The value or purchasing power of money is the amount of goods and services a unit of money will buy. This "value" is constantly changing in relation to many factors. Simply stated, when costs go up, the value of the dollar goes down. This inverse relationship means that higher prices lower the value of the dollar because more dollars are needed to obtain the same amount of goods or services.

When banks in the Federal Reserve System create money out of thin air, they are introducing more (worthless) dollars into the system. Following this delusion, that means more dollars are chasing the same assets as the value of the dollar drops even further. The effect is that workers work even harder and end up getting paid less because what they are paid with has a dwindling value.

Real money, backed by real commodities or products, would only be possible if there were no market interventions, price controls, or direct influence on the money supply. By allowing the power brokers in Washington to influence the money supply, our nation was destined to follow the great societies of the past that eventually collapsed under their own weight.

There has been a decline in economic stability since the Federal Reserve System became effective. The publicized reason for the instability has been bad decision making on the part of the Federal Reserve Board. It has been argued that economic instability had been more of product of monetary mismanagement than any other destabilizing economic force. But, we must ask ourselves, who is it that bore the brunt of economic instability? The common man! The bankers and politicians (lawyers) have reaped fat rewards, and even government itself has grown exponentially. The actions taken by the Federal Reserve exacerbate the market changes and cause the financial ruin of millions of Americans. This, it is argued, is by intentional design.

All levels of the public sector seemingly have extended their reach into the pockets of households and businesses by instituting more and more taxes and fees in order to raise the money to pay for all of the projects, programs and services they have promised. Giving and promising so much to the people, yet unable or unwilling to curtail spending in other areas, has led to large yearly budget deficits and mounting debt.

Financing government operations and providing for programs has only been possible through borrowing money and/or raising taxes. At all levels of government, in order to pay for large capital projects, programs, or to make up for shortfalls in revenue, they have raised money through the sale of debt securities.

THE UNITED STATES TREASURY

Government bonds function the same as corporate bonds in that they have a face (par) value, pay a set interest rate and promise repayment of the par value on the date of maturity. Governments or government agencies sell their bonds to all the other sectors. These bonds can take many forms, but government bonds simply represent loans to the different government entities that make up the public sector.

Through the United States Treasury, the Federal Government sells long, medium and short-term debt securities. Not only are these bonds used to finance projects, functions and operations of the government, but they are also used to manipulate interest rates and monetary policy with the coordinated effort of the Federal Reserve.

The Congress of the United States controls spending and budgetary matters, which includes the level of debt the Country, by law, is allowed to take on. The Federal Government spends most of its money on entitlements (social welfare programs) and national defense. Another large portion is committed to servicing the national debt. After veteran's affairs, education, commerce and transportation, only a small percentage of federal spending is allocated for other projects.

Because of recent wars and the financial crisis that started in 2008, the level of spending has increased dramatically in many areas. This has forced the federal government to sell more bonds than ever before to fund it all.

It is important to understand the function and results of the actions of the United States Treasury. United States Government Bonds, like other government and corporate bonds, trade freely on the open market where individuals, other governments, corporations and financial institutions can buy and sell these debt instruments. These are also backed by the full faith and credit of the United States. As such, like currency, they are worthless in real value but there are those who believe in their value. The government sells their bonds at a very low interest rate, relative to the private debt market as a whole. The effective yield on the Treasury bonds is the standard by which the pricing of all other bonds are set.

FREE TRADE/INTERNATIONAL TRADE

It is through free trade that the world can achieve a more efficient allocation of resources. It is only through unencumbered commerce can a freeman earn the wages he deserves for the products he produces. Promulgating free trade, however, is difficult to establish and maintain. With the political forces in power today, it may seem impossible to achieve. The government has to be expelled from commerce and economic freedom can be achieved through honest, hard work. To dispense with those who have violated the Constitution would also deal with the merchants, bankers and lawyers. Doing away with their rule of law (that only benefits them), the commercial law in its current form and the merchant law would take this nation much close to the freedom we seek and deserve.

Our trading partners have to exchange meaningful products or use a currency backed by actual commodities — something of substance. It would have to be a medium of exchange that could not be manipulated or altered. In other words, the government could not borrow in our name to manipulate markets, nor could bankers create money out of thin air. A currency would thus retain its value and be in accord with pure barter and trade. Imagine the cost savings in products if there were no taxes or no interest payments due on the products, facilities and capital used to create the products! With no bankers or merchants taking their undeserved cut, prices of all goods and services would drop accordingly.

Thanks to President Roosevelt, it is currently illegal to conduct transactions (create a value-based currency) outside of the scope of the system that is currently in place. Why? Because if such a currency was created, the government and bankers would lose control of commerce. They could not impose their taxes and fees. They could not regulate markets. The value of their fiat money would drop to nothing against a

41

manipulation-free currency and they (the politicians, bankers and lawyers) would lose control of the people.

The system currently in place has erected huge barriers of free trade and entry into markets. Beyond taxes and regulations, there are also fees, legal requirements, zoning laws, licenses, protective tariffs and quotas. These are simply an excise tax on goods and are not only imposed for purposes of collecting revenue for the government but also restricting commerce. The additional cost raises the price of goods. Quotas specify the maximum amounts of specific commodities (or facilities) which may be produced during a given period of time. With any regulation or price controls in place, how is it that we as a people live in a free-market economy? We are, in effect, paying more to support and for the privilege of the elite to control over our lives.

These government imposed tools to restrict trade are used for a variety of reasons: but "special interests" tops the list. In order to advance free trade amongst ourselves -- within our own shores - we must take steps to change the course of history.

A CHANGE IN GOVERNMENT:

First, as an American, it is incumbent upon us to change the system. Do not believe either of the two major political parties who have held a strangle-hold over our country for way too long. Both parties are the opposite side of the same coin and serve for one purpose, simply to stay in power.

Taking responsibility for our own destiny, means to never vote for an official who has held a political office. They have already been corrupted. Instead, encourage citizens in your own community to run for office. Choose freemen who share the desire for self-determination and economic freedom, encourage them and support them -- but hold them to their word to exact the needed changes. They must support the Constitution as written and act to repeal all laws passed beyond the scope of the powers enumerated in the Constitution. If that person you support gets elected, hold them to their word and if they stray, vote in someone else. There can be no loyalty to a political party-only loyalty to truth.

Taking responsibility for our own destiny also means to reject the Babylonian System. Do not borrow money to buy anything. Do not use credit cards. If you cannot afford something, go without. Learn a skill or a trade where you are able to manufacture or produce something of value.

Rely on your own skills and abilities to advance in your field. Opt out of Social Security and Medicare and save for your own retirement. Simply living within your means and avoiding the interest payments for car loans, mortgages and credit cards (and saving the money) will double your wealth in seven years.

Organize an economic exchange community. Find doctors, dentists along with farmers, carpenters and other craftsmen willing to barter for their services. Whenever possible, trade your skill or craft for whatever goods, products or services you need and do not exchange worthless paper money.

READER'S GLOSSARY:

In order to fully understand the meaning of everything written in this chapter, it is necessary to gain a full appreciation of the terms used. <u>Some</u> of the vocabulary in this chapter are "words of art". In other words, they have a common everyday meaning that we all know but also a meaning that has a very specific, special connotation. These definitions cannot be found in a regular dictionary. Instead, one must locate and utilize a Black's Law Dictionary. An avid reader would take the time to look up the definitions in a regular dictionary and then in the Black's Law Dictionary to compare and contrast the differences. Once the reader of this chapter looks up and understands the true, legal definitions of some of the below listed words, many of the arguments and discussions in this chapter will become clearer.

It is the reader's responsibility to look up and fully understand the definitions of the following words:

ACCESSION

ADHESION

ARTIFICIAL

ATORN

ATTORNEY

BANK PLENRY

BAR

BARON

CHARTER

CIVIL

CONFEDERATION

CONFISCATION

DELEGATES

DEMOCRACY

ENTITY

FIAT

FREEMAN

JOINT

IMPEACH

INALIENABLE

INVOKE

MARQUEE

MAXIMS

MONEY

PARLIAMENT

PRINCIPLE

REGAIN

REPRESENTATIVE

REPUBLIC

RESOLUTION

REVOLUTION

SECURE

SENATE

SINE DIE

STATE

TITLE

THE MONEY SUPPLY, KEYNESIAN AND MONETARIST THEORY

"Money, one of the truly great inventions of man, constitutes a most fascinating aspect of economic science." (Federal Reserve Bank of Philadelphia, "Creeping Inflation," Business Review, August 1957, P. 3.)

Money, monetary policy and interest rates are prominent subjects in economics. Money is actually the most crucial element in economic science because it functions as more than simply a passive tool which facilitates the economy's operation. The monetary system is the lifeblood of the circular flow of income and expenditure. The supply of money effects many aspects of our economy including supply, demand, interest rates, inflation along with many other facets. These factors all relate to whether our economy is functioning properly or not. Over the years, several major economic theories relating to monetary policy have been debated and implemented with varying results: Classical Economics, Keynesian Economics, Supply Side Economics and Monetarism. These "schools of economic thought," when implemented, have had a direct impact on levels of output, employment and prices. Money, specifically the supply of money, has been a driving force in our economic system.

There are various functions of money. Primarily, money is a means of exchange that can be used in buying and selling goods and services. Money is also a standard of value, what society uses as a "measuring stick" to determine the relative worth of various goods and services. Stating prices using one common standard allows consumers to simply and easily compare the relative worth of many commodities. finally, money serves as a store of value, because it is the most liquid of all assets, i.e., it can be directly exchanged for goods and services. Other assets such as commodities, must be sold first, or used in complicated barter.

Because of the many uses of money, there is demand for it. People need money as a medium of exchange, or transactional demand. Money allows people and businesses to easily conduct transactions to meet their needs. The basic determination of transactional demand for money is the level of Gross National Product (GNP). The larger the amount of all goods and services exchanged in the economy, the more money needed to negotiate these transactions.

The second factor that creates demand for money is asset demand. People hold their assets and seek to retain the value of those assets in various forms. Beyond the actual currency itself, money is used to procure all other asset classes. There can be a cost associated with holding money if interest rates are high and people who are adverse to seeing the value of their money decline seek to invest it in asset classes that have rising values. The asset demand for money, therefore moves in the opposite direction of interest rates. In other words, higher interest rates reduces the demand for money as people shift into other asset classes. Lower interest rates increase the demand for money.

In our economy, "money" can have either a narrow or broad definition. The term "M1" is used to define money in a narrow sense, and it is composed of coins, paper money, and demand deposits. Coins and paper money are usually simply called currency. Our currency is "fiat money" in that it has little to no intrinsic value but is instead backed by the full faith and credit of the United States Government. Currency is a debt of our government, whereas demand deposits are a debt to banks.

The broader definition of money is called "M2" and that includes the elements of M1 along with time deposits and some government bonds. Although not as liquid as currency, these additional elements of money are nearly as liquid and thus included in the broader definition of money. These definitions and distinctions are important in that in order to set monetary policy, or to maintain stable growth, economists look to the supply and demand of money in order to direct policy. It can be shown that changes in interest rates and causes of inflation are directly related to the money supply. Money derives its value from scarcity, a phenomenon of supply and demand.

The real value or purchasing power of money is the amount of goods and services a unit of money will buy. This "value" is constantly changing in relation to many factors. Simply stated, when costs go up, the value of the dollar goes down. This inverse relationship means that higher prices lower the value of the dollar because more dollars are needed to obtain the same amount of goods or services.

In the several competing theories concerning monetary policy, the goal has always been the same; to foster stable growth, inflation, and full employment. Within these theories are basic equations that attempt to explain the interaction between the money supply and our economy. Keynesian economics focuses upon the aggregate demand of all goods and services and its components. The equation is expressed as C+I+G=NNP means that consumption expenditures of households plus gross private domestic investment plus government purchase of goods and services is equal to the Net National Product (NWP). The expenditures approach measures the money spent on all finished or final goods and services.

Another economic theory, based on the philosophy of monetarism, uses a different model to explain and predict the effect of monetary policy. In the Equation of Exchange: MV=PQ, the supply of money (M), when multiplied by the velocity of money (V), is equal to the price of goods and service (P) times the volume of goods and services. The velocity of money is defined as the number of times per year a dollar is spent on final goods and services. For example, if there was $1 trillion in the money supply and the NNP was $5 trillion, the velocity of money would be 5.

The difference between these two models is that the quantitative method puts much less emphasis on the money supply. Conversely, the Equation of Exchange states that the supply of money has a much broader, direct impact on total output, which in turn effects the entire economy. Despite their differences, Doth models are useful and can be insightful. By definition, the two models can even be combined. Because MV (supply of money times the velocity of money) is equal to the total amount spent on goods in one year, it is the same as C+I+G. NNP (Net National Product) and MV are equivalent terms. Using substitution, we can state that NNP = PQ.

Using historical data, each competing theory has tried to validate their methodology and determine the best current and future policy as it relates to money supply and how to best allow our economy to flourish. Because the several models did not fully explain every economic situation, other theories have come into play. From Classical Economic Theory, through Keynesian Economics and with the advent of Supply Side Economics, policy makers and their economic teams attempt to stabilize the business cycles, dampen inflation, while efficiently utilizing the means of production and creating full employment.

In Classical Economic Theory, the basis was that capitalism was capable of providing virtually uninterrupted full employment. Some of the most notable classical economists were John Stuart Mill, F. Y. Edgeworth, Alfred Marshall, and A.C. Pigou. They felt that the price system alone was capable of providing for full employment of all of the economy's resources. But, even they acknowledged that during abnormal circumstances such as wars, political upheavals, and droughts, the economy would be pushed away from full employment. However, it was their position that after those deviations occurred, automatic adjustments within the price system would restore the economy to full employment.

The classical economists did not believe in or condone market intervention, price controls, or direct influence on the money supply. This "Laissez Faire" approach later became the keystone for the monetarist's view of economic theory. The classical theory of employment was based on two positions: 1) that underspending would be unlikely to occur; and, 2) even if a deficiency of total spending were to arise, price-wage adjustments would occur so as to insure that a decline in total spending would not create declines in real output, employment and real incomes.

The classical economist's denial of the possibility of underspending was based on the acceptance of Say's Law. Say's Law simply states that producing goods generates an amount of income that is exactly equal to the value of goods produced. Stated another way, supply creates its own demand. When something is produced, using this theory, it was believed that the exact same amount was automatically generated to take that output off of the market. The circular flow model of the economy suggests this proposition is somewhat accurate. However, there are missing elements that invalidate Say's Law--the main factor being that the income produced from creating output must be spent on output. Say's Law failed to account for savings.

Because there is no guarantee that the wage income derived from production output would be spent and not saved, and there was no way to forecast the savings rate, Say's Law did not accurately portray the economic cycle. The savings was thus deemed "leakage" that undermined the operation of Say's Law. The savings of households that did not go toward the purchase of goods and services would draw away from the amount being spent, and therefore supply did not create its own demand. The result would be unsold goods, cutbacks in production and unemployment.

Classical economists countered that every dollar saved would be reinvested by businesses and therefore would increase demand, just from a different economic sector. They argued that the money markets would guarantee an equality of savings and investments that would fill the consumption gap left by savings. It seemed plausible in that the effect of savings on the interest rate would spur businesses into investing in growth opportunities with cheap capital, hence absorbing the money and putting it to use. Also, the argument was advanced that low interest rates would compel households to spend rather than to save, since there was little incentive to save. Interest rates, classical economists believed, were the self-regulating mechanism that would insure that dollars saved would be then utilized by businesses seeking to expand using money borrowed at low interest rates. Through the money markets, an equilibrium for interest rates would be reached.

The second argument of the classical economist was that price-wage flexibility would guarantee full employment. They argued that the level of output that can be sold depends not only on the level of total spending, but also on the level of production prices. Simply stated, a decline in spending would be offset by a decline in prices. Even with savings, the decline in total spending, they argued, would not result in declining production, lower real incomes or effect the level of employment. The necessary variable was that prices would have to decline in proportion to the decline in expenditures.

Also, it was theorized that competition among sellers would ensure price flexibility. As demand for products dropped, competing producers would lower their prices to dispose of inventory. Lower prices would increase the value of the dollar and would permit people who did not save the ability to get more for their money. In essence, they argued the supply/

demand market influences, in and of themselves, would make saving a benefit.

The obvious shortcoming of this argument was that in order for a Business to stay profitable, the cost of resources would also have to go down. In order to reduce the cost of production, a business would have to cut wages. In arguing the classical position, they stated that wage decreases were inevitable, as were higher levels of unemployment as demand receded. However, they felt that at the lower rates of wages, producers would be more willing to hire, thus absorbing the unutilized labor. Competition for jobs by the unemployed would compel labor to accept jobs at lower wags level. Again, the classical economists relied on supply and demand in that eventually there would be an equilibrium wage where full employment was profitable for businesses and workers. It was felt that anyone willing to work at the new, lower wage level could find a job.

Several factors came into play that the classical economists failed to account for in their analysis. First, they never considered voluntary unemployment was possible, i.e., that workers would not work at lower wages. Second, their theory did not account for productivity gains, wherein fewer employees through technological advances, were able to create the same output as a larger workforce. Productivity gains made it unprofitable to hire workers at any wage since the required output that could be sold was being produced by fewer people.

The Great Depression showed that capitalism, with its price system adjustments, was not capable of creating a self-regulating mechanism that would insure full employment. The classical school of economics belief was that government assistance in the economy was harmful. This was countered by looking at how our economy functioned in a different way. This came about because there were long periods of high unemployment and inflation. During the 1930's economists started to criticize the underlying premises of classical economic theory.

In 1936 English economist John Maynard Keynes articulated his theories concerning the level of employment in capitalistic economies in his work, "General Theory of Employment, Interest, and Money." It was Keynes's work that shattered the underpinnings of classical economic theory and launched a revolution in economic thought.

The major contribution of Keynes's work was to dispel the theory that capitalism was capable of guaranteeing full employment through market mechanisms. He argued that it was possible for the economy to reach an aggregate output equilibrium with a high level of unemployment or high inflation. If that equilibrium was reached, market forces were useless in absorbing the unemployed resources and they would sit idle. He went on to posit that full employment and stable prices could only happen by chance. Finally, the forwarded the idea that economic depressions were not just caused by wars, droughts or other abnormal circumstances, but also by internal economic factors that were not accounted for in prior economic theories. He argued that fundamental economic decisions, internal factors such as the savings rate and investment decisions, played a much more significant role in capitalism.

Keynesian theory rejected Say's Law because it questioned the ability of interest rates to find an equilibrium between savings and investment. The key to this was the logical conclusion that if people were saving more and spending less, why would businesses borrow money to expand as their products went unsold and inventories increased? It was common sense that reduced demand could not lead to an investment that would increase production.

Furthermore, Keynes pointed out that the classical concept of the money markets were oversimplified. He pointed out that savings was not the only source of financing for investments. The money held by households as savings represented accumulated wealth. These funds could be drawn on and then invested directly by the household.

When banks use personal savings to offer loans, they add to the money supply, subject to the multiplier effect. Bank lending is therefore another means of augmenting investment. As a result, a decrease in the savings of households and less bank lending can mean an increase in investments. This tended to further undermine Say's Law. Keynes determined that output, employment and price levels can fluctuate because an excess of investment over savings results in an increase in total spending, which has an expansionary impact on the economy. Conversely, an increase in savings over investment would lead to contraction in the economy.

Savings and investments can be at odds and thereby nave a direct impact on total output, employment, total income and price levels. He was able to show that there was no way to insure that savings and investments would find an equilibrium through interest rates. Using this model, Keynes put much of the first proposition of Say's Law to rest.

Keynes also discredited the classical economic view of price-wage flexibility. He argued that the flexibility necessary to adjust for a decline in total spending simply did not exist. The reason for this was that the price system in capitalism was not and could never be purely competitive.

Market imperfections, along with practical and political obstacles worked against price-wage flexibility.

There were monopolistic producers which dominated several important markets. These monopolies had the ability and the will to resist falling prices as demand declined. At the same time, strong labor unions could be equally determined to fight wage deflation. Politicians, who set minimum wages, were equally aware and sensitive to the ramifications of allowing wages to drop. Finally, the public at large was resistant to being paid less than reasonable wages or at rates that were lower than customary. On the other side, some employers would be hesitant to cut wages because that would tend to reduce productivity and lower morale.

It was during the Great Depression that Keynesian economic theory started to take hold. With massive unemployment and the world's economies in free-fall, there was evidence that declines in real wages did not reduce the level of unemployment. There were people willing to work for scraps of food, but there was no work to be had. That was the result of there being no demand for some goods and services, leaving no reason and no means for employers to hire.

If lower prices and wages decline, Keynes reasoned, that necessarily meant lower incomes and a reduction in total spending. The obvious conclusion was that lower wages and prices would not reduce unemployment. It was, he determined, classical economists being caught in the fallacy of composition. The proposition that wage-price flexibility may work at one firm where the workers purchase the same amount of their output at lower prices with lower wages, did not apply to the economy as a whole. His reasoning was that wages are the major source of income for most families and the economy. Across-the-board declines in wages could only lead to declines in incomes which leads to less demand and then even lower production. Lower production would then lead to further job losses and even higher unemployment.

By rejecting the classical economic theory, that there is no automatic mechanism to bring about full employment, it set the tone in this nation to revise its approach to both monetary policy and fiscal policy. It was determined that the amount of goods and services produced and the level of employment depend directly on the level of total spending or "aggregate demand".

During the Depression, Keynsian thought played a major role in determining a course of action in order to stabilize the economy. Governmental fiscal actions, it was determined, can have an important stabilizing effect. After World War II, when it seemed as if the same problems encountered during the Great Depression were developing, Congress passed the Employment Act of 1946. In that act, they set forth the groundwork wherein the Federal Government was empowered to take positive actions through fiscal and monetary policy in order to maintain economic stability.

One of the tools used was discretionary fiscal policy. That is the deliberate manipulation of taxes and government spending by Congress to offset cyclical fluctuations in output and employment and stimulating economic growth. Using the formula C+I+G=NNP, it is clear to see that an increase in government aiding will boost the aggregate demand, thus increasing the net national product. Similarly, a reduction in taxes would make more money available for purchases of goods and service. The effect would be to increase the NNP as personal spending increased. An increase in taxes with a concurrent increased government spending should initially nave no effect on NNP, while the government has the ability to redistribute the wealth or spend on projects for the public good. However, through the multiplier effect, eventually that public spending will increase NNP.

The process of taxation and spending by the government can be extremely complicated. The effect are delayed and have ramifications in other sectors of the economy. There are many variables such as deficit spending and the method by which public spending is financed. There is no question that fiscal policy can and does have a direct impact on the economy as a whole. Whether it is stabilizing and beneficial or not is still a topic of debate. One of the biggest debates after the level of taxation is about when the government creates money to pay its Dills or fund projects. These questions are where Keynesian economists and monetarists clash.

With the creation of the Federal Reserve, the Board of Governors has the responsibility of controlling the operation of our monetary and banking systems. "The fundamental objective of monetary policy is to assist the economy in achieving a full-employment, noninflationary level of total output." Basically, monetary policy concerns altering the nation's money supply in order to stabilize the economy, foster growth and keep inflation in check.

Policies based upon the Keynsian theories, and in use since the 1940's, are quite diverse. Through the Federal Reserve's Board of Governors, certain control techniques are used to influence the size of member bank's reserves. Because excess reserves are what is used to expand the money supply through lending, any manipulation of excess reserves has a direct impact on the money supply. This is a function of the amounts commercial banks can and are willing to lend at certain interest rates. Interest rates are determined by the supply of money. Changes in the supply of money will effect interest rates and the amount of credit bankers are willing to make available to borrowers.

It was theorized that changes in the cost and availability of loans has a direct impact on the spending habits of society. It also has an impact on the investment decisions of individuals and businesses. That, in tarn, has an impact on the level of output, employment, income, and prices. We have seen this in effect since this country has fallen into a deep recession in late 2008. The Federal Reserve has Kept interest rates as low as possible in order to try and increase production, reduce unemployment and get the economy stable. Along with massive spending by Congress (fiscal policy) and the utilization of many tools the Federal Reserve has to spur growth, the economy has since stabilized.

The Keynesian model of aggregate demand puts much less emphasis on the money supply. It is believed that there are many loose links in the cause and effect chain of events associated with monetary policy. Therefore the Keynesians feel that the tools used by the Federal Reserve used in order to stabilize the economy are uncertain, unreliable and can lead to unintended consequences.

Economists have learned that monetary policy imposed by the Federal Reserve may have several predictable consequences. For example, the investment component of total spending is more likely than consumer spending to be effected by changes in interest rates. They have found that interest rates seem to have little impact on whether consumers decide whether to save or spend. This has once again been proven as recently as the first quarter of 2009. With interest rates at historic lows, consumers have increased their rate of savings and did not spend more. Conversely, higher interest rates in the past aid not seem to tamper borrowing since monthly payments could remain the same by lengthening the duration of the loan.

In the business sector, however, there seems to be a much closer correlation between interest rates and spending. Since capital investments for property, plants, and equipment are very expensive, and have long durations, lower interest rates compel business to borrow more and invest more. That saves them from paying higher debt service, or higher interest rates in the future. From the perspective of businesses, it saves them a great deal of money to borrow and invest when interest rates are low. It is for this reason that interest rates have a more obvious impact on investments.

Keynesians believe that capitalism suffers from inherent shortcomings. The market system does not provide for public goods, it misallocates resources where externalities and monopolies exist, and it yields a highly unequal distribution of income. This school of economic thought believes that government does and should play an active role in stabilizing the economy. Through the use of fiscal and monetary policies, the government can smooth out the economic cycles. Keynesians believe that fiscal policy, i.e., the manipulation of taxes and public spending, should be the main tools used to influence the economy.

Milton Friedman, from the University of Chicago, and the winner of the 197G Nobel Prize in Economics, has espoused and put forth a different philosophy. Friedman is the intellectual leader behind the monetarists. Basically, they assert that the role of money is much greater in determining the level of economic output that Keynesians believe. Much like the classical economists, the monetarists believe in a laissez faire market orientation. Through research they have tried to show that the competitive marketplace does, in fact, automatically allocate resources efficiently. This school of economic thought asserts that governmental decision making is fraught with bureaucratic inefficiencies that are harmful to individuals. They frequently point to policy mistakes and that centralized government control eventually leads to the loss of individual freedom. (Milton Friedman, Capitalism and Freedom, Chicago: The University of Chicago Press, 1962.)

The monetarist's view is that the economy would provide stability and full employment if it were not for the intervention and interference of the government. For example, monetarists believe that wage-price flexibility would work if the government did not set a minimum wage, did not advance pro-union legislation or provide price supports for agricultural goods. There are other differences between Keynsians and monetarists. They take opposing views when it comes to the public and private sectors. Keynsian thought is that private investment is what causes the economy to be unstable and that the government provides important stabilization mechanisms. To the monetarist, the government creates rigidities which weaken the ability of market forces to provide stability. The tools used by government, although well intended, aggravate the instability they are meant to fix.

The monetarists feel that monetary policy and the money supply are much more important in determining the level of economic activity than do the Keynesians. In fact, monetarists believe that changes in the money supply are the single, most important factor in determining the level of output, employment and prices. They state that there is a direct link between the supply of money and economic activity.

Their analysis is contingent on the fact that the velocity of money is stable, or nearly stable. As stated earlier, the velocity of money is the number of times per year the average dollar is spent on finished goods and services. If velocity is constant, or nearly constant, any increase in the money supply will either increase the price of goods, quantity of goods, or both. Using the combined equations $MV=NNP$ the theory states that an increase in the money supply with a constant velocity of money will increase the Net National Product.

Whether an increase in the money supply effects the price of goods or quantity of goods depends on whether the economy is in a recession or is enjoying full employment. If the economy is in a deep recession, an increase in the money supply will increase the total quantity of goods produced. The increased output would compel firms to hire and would bring the economy closer to full employment. Conversely, if the economy is already at full employment, an increase in the money supply would lead to higher prices, as the quantity of total output would become a constant. As the economy reaches maximum output, or full employment, the price and quantity can both rise with an increase in the money supply.

The critical question thus becomes if the velocity of money is stable. Contrary to the monetarist's view, Keynesians believe it is not stable. If it is stable, a 10% increase in the money supply would lead to a 10% increase in the NNP. If the velocity of money is variable, then **the** link between the increase of the money supply and the Net National Product is loose and uncertain.

To buttress their argument that the velocity of money is stable, monetarists view money as primarily a medium of exchange with only transactional demand. They do not believe there is an asset demand associated with money. In that, they assert the. amount of money the public will hold depends on the volume of transactions, or, in other terms, the Net National Product. It is their view that spending will simply increase until NNP has increased to the point where there is an equilibrium.

Keynesians respond that there is variability in the velocity of money. The assertion is couched on the assumption that there is a demand for money as an asset. The amount of money that is held as an asset, which is not used for transactions, therefore has a velocity of zero because it is never spent.

One can extrapolate this out to the situation in relation to U.S. public debt. China currently holds approximately $700 billion worth of United States Treasury bills, bonds and notes. Assuming a combined interest rate of 4% on all of their holdings, the United States Treasury must pay $28 billion dollars in interest to China every year. Assuming China does not spend any of the interest income, what is the velocity of that $28 billion dollars? It would sit idle, and be zero. Luckily for our government, China reinvests that money into more United States debt instruments.

However, if China chose to spend that interest income on any specific segment of our economy, making the velocity of that money equal the velocity of transaction money, the impact would be felt immediately. Even though monetarists believe there is no asset demand for money, China's asset horde could immediately undercut that assumption. Or, if they sold off all of their holdings and invested the money in the private sector, there would be rampant inflation and severe devaluation of the dollar.

China holding such a mass reserve has the effect of lowering the over-all velocity of money. In addition, their reserve of foriegn currency is such that it could alter the money supply, which could theoretically be a detriment to the United States.

Keynesians view the velocity of money in a much more sophisticated way, tying in the effect of interest rates on savings and investments. In the extreme case where all of an increase in the money supply is held by the public as additional asset balances, i.e., if they hoarded the money and use none of it for transactions, the velocity would decrease and there would be no effect at all in NNP. The relative importance of asset demand for money varies with the interest rate in an inverse relationship. The lower the interest rate, the higher the demand for money. That means an increase in the money supply would tend to lower interest rates and since it would be less expensive to hold money, more of it would be held in zero-velocity assets.

This scenario more closely resembles the actions taken by society during this latest financial crisis. Even with low interest rates, households have hoarded money in savings; while at the same time the money supply has been dramatically increased. It has taken more than increasing the money supply to help the American economy recover from a steep recession. Increasing the money supply drastically, in and of itself, did not (as of yet) lead directly to a proportional increase in NNP. That can be partially explained by the velocity of money declining because households are not spending and businesses are not investing.

The same argument can be made concerning the recent fiscal policy, where Congress allocated $700 billion dollars in the T&RP program in order to "bailout" the banking system. When these funds were allocated, it was believed that banks would use these funds to secure their balance sheets and free up capital for more lending. The credit crisis was not solved through providing billions of dollars to individual firms. Instead, these major financial institutions did not ease credit as expected and instead hoarded the money by redepositing the funds into the Federal Reserve System. The bailout money did prevent the collapse of several ailing financial institutions and prevented a run on the banks. But, it took even more action by the Federal Reserve and more stimulus from a massive spending bill passed by Congress to somewhat ease the credit crunch.

It seems evident that in a steep recession, no matter what tools are used, or what combination: be it fiscal stimulus, manipulation of interest rates, capital injections, increases in the money supply; the outcome is unknown. Though Ben Bernanke, Chairman of the Federal Reserve, has recently announced that the economy is recovering, (Wall Street Journal, 8/20/09) the economic situation remains tenuous. With unemployment near 10%, and households unsure about the security of future earnings, consumers are still not spending. When society starts to spend money, shifting from holding money as an asset to transactional demand, it will be interesting to see what effect this has on the velocity of money, NNP, interest rates, and inflation.

From the Keynesian perspective, velocity varies directly with the rate of interest and inversely with the supply of money. That means that the tight relationship between the money supply and NNP, as espoused by monetarists, does not exist. Because of many variables, and how statistics are viewed, it is very difficult to determine which school of economic thought is correct on this issue. Monetarists point to the past close correlation between the money supply and money GNP as evidence to support their position that velocity is stable. Conversely, Keynesians argue that the velocity of money is unstable and can vary cyclically and secularly. They can show through historical data that the velocity of money has varied between 2 and 5 over the past 75 years.

It should be noted that even a small change in velocity, using either the Keynesian model or the Equation of Exchange, can have a dramatic affect on total output, employment, incomes and prices. An element that does not factor into either equation, but seems to effect on the velocity of money, is consumer confidence. If households feel secure in their jobs, in the economy as a whole, there are more likely to spend more. Measuring consumer confidence has become a staple for economists because increased consumer spending means the economy will expand. It is difficult to measure the psychology of consumers and the effect of fiscal or monetary policy changes. It can be argued that velocity of money is a variable dependent upon the attitude of consumers. Even if the attitude of consumers is effected by policy, job security carries a greater weight. Any sense of job security, by definition, requires near full employment of resources in a more localized, secular sense. Discounting the attitude of the consumer would seem to be a big mistake.

Economic stability, measured growth, near full-employment, and low inflation can be best brought about, Keynes argued, through fiscal policy, not monetary policy. Monetarists felt that manipulating taxation and spending does more harm than good. They contended that tax increases meant to create greater income equality reduces the incentive to work, invest and bear risk. The effect would be to reduce the total national income.

Also, monetarists argued that public spending is usually for dubious projects and government used resources that would be more efficiently used by the private sector. Finally, monetarists posited that fiscal policy was weak and ineffective because of the crowding-out effect. They believed that by borrowing for public spending, the government is competing with private enterprises for funds and the borrowing raises interest rates. The net effect, it was felt, was that any increase in government spending was offset by declines in investments.

As Milton Friedman said:

"...in my opinion, the state of the budget by itself has no significant effect on the course of nominal [money] income, on inflation, on deflation, or on cyclical fluctuations." (Statement by Friedman in Milton Friedman and Walter Heller, Monetary vs Fiscal Policy sw York: W. W. Norton S Co., Inc., 1969), p. 51.)

Monetarists pointed out that if deficit spending was financed through creation of money, the crowding-out effect would not occur, but the economic impact would be through the mechanism of the increase in the money supply, not fiscal policy. Keynesians agree that deficits financed by creating new money would have a greater stimulating effect than by borrowing. However, they deny that the crowding-out effect from deficit spending through borrowing has as much of a impact as monetarists assert. Keynesians believe that a small increase in interest rates would only result in a small decrease in the investment component of aggregate demand.

Monetarists have a low regard for fiscal policy and advocate stabilization of the economy through monetary policy. However, they do not believe that cyclical changes should be countered using the tools of "loosening" or "tightening" monetary policy.

Loosening and tightening has been the method the Federal Reserve has used to influence the economy. Setting target interest rates has been their primary tool. When banks deposit funds with the Fed, the Fed pays them interest. This is a recent development because in the past, the Fed did not pay interest on reserves. In addition, the Fed sets a target rate that banks pay to each other for short-term loans. By lowering the interest rate, there is less of an incentive (less profit potential for banks) to deposit funds into the Federal Reserve or to loan money to another bank. Banks then have the profit incentive to loan money and take on more risk. What interest rates banks charge consumers has a direct correlation to the Federal Reserve's manipulation of the rates they pay and the target rates they set.

For borrowers, lower interest rates and more money available makes it easier to get loans and it costs them less. Thus, maintaining low target rates is termed a "loose" monetary policy, because loans are cheaper and easier to obtain. The availability of credit at low rates increases the demand for goods and services.

Conversely, when there is too much growth and inflation is a problem, the Federal Reserve can raises the interest rates they pay banks, and the rates banks can charge each other. The effect of more money being put into reserve, where the banks earn a guaranteed rate of return, and it decreases the amount of money being loaned. The less money there is to loan, the harder it is to get a loan, and the more expensive it is to borrow money. This results in less economic activity. Raising interest rates is called "tightening", because it is harder to get loans.

In addition to manipulating interest rates, the Federal Reserve can also increase or decrease the percentage of deposits member banks are required to hold in reserve. This function enables the Federal Reserve to manipulate the overall money supply.

Another tool at the Federal Reserve's disposal in order to tighten or loosen the money supply is the buying and selling of Treasury bills, bonds and notes. The Federal Government, through the United States Treasury, borrows money and the Federal Reserve buys some of the debt instruments (loans the money) and holds the securities. In times of inflation, to reduce the amount of money in the money supply, the Federal Reserve can sell the Treasury bonds it holds to the public (individuals, firms, and foreign governments). The money they take in from the sale of the bonds has the effect of reducing the amount of money in the economy. During recessionary times, the Fed does the opposite -- they buy bonds from the public, paying out cash and increasing the money supply.

Monetarists argue that there has been a decline in economic stability since the Federal Reserve System became effective. In their view, the reason for the instability has been bad decision making on the part of the Federal Reserve Board. Monetarists argued that economic instability had been more of product of monetary mismanagement than any other destabilizing economic force. One reasons for the mismanagement, it was claimed, was that there is a time lag between Federal Reserve action and economic impact. Before monetary policies had time to influence the economy, the economy would have corrected on its own. The action taken by the Fed would therefore exacerbate the market changes beyond what was intended. In other words, a "loose" monetary policy would kick in only after a cyclical recovery had already started and the additional money supply would push the economy into an inflationary situation. Or, "tightening" at the peak of an expansion would come into play as the economy slowed of its own accord, pushing the economy into a recession.

Using empirical data, Friedman showed that a change in the money supply would alter the NNP in a span as short as six to eight months or as long as two years later. Because of this uncertainty, he argued that it was impossible to predict the effect of a change in monetary policy or how to decide the direction.

Friedman also argued that the Fed was mistaken in relying on the levels of interest rates to determine policy. Pointing to the effect of a full-employment economy that is growing, with the demand for money high, interest rates would rise. If the Federal Reserve Board reasoned their job was to stabilize interest rates, they would embark on a policy to loosen the money supply in order to bring interest rates down. The net effect, Friedman reasoned, would be an inflationary spiral. Or, during a recession, with interest rates falling, the Fed might tighten in order to bring interest rates up, thus exacerbating the recession.

The monetarist's solution was The Monetary Rule. Friedman advocated that monetary authorities should not attempt to stabilize interest rates but instead should stabilize the money supply. Instead of a discretionary monetary policy, he suggested legislation that would automatically expand the money supply each year at the same annual rate as the potential growth of the Gross National Product (GMP). His sugestion was that the money supply should be increased 3-5% without discretion.

"Such a rule, it is claimed, would eliminate the major cause of instability in the economy--the capricious and unpredictable impact of countercyclical monetary policy. As long as the money supply grows at a constant rate each year, be it 3, 4, 5 percent, any decline into recession will only be temporary. The liquidity provided by a constantly growing money supply will cause aggregate demand to expand. Similarly, if the supply of money does not rise at a more than average rate, any inflationary increase in spending will burn itself out for lack of fuel." L.S. Ritter and W.L. Silber, Money, 2d. Ed. (New York: Basic Books, Inc., 1973, pp. 134-35.)

Theoretically and realistically speaking, the Monetary Rule fell flat. As Keynesians pointed out, because the velocity of money was historically volatile, contrary to the assumption of monetarists, a constant annual increase in the money supply would contribute to extreme fluctuations in aggregate demand and actually promote economic instability as the economy bounced around to establish an equilibrium. With no discretion,, monetary authorities would be unable to react to externalities or internal gyrations.

Furthermore, policy makers realized that the Monetary Rule would leave them impotent and they would be forced to "stand on the sidelines" as the economy floundered. If the Monetary Rule was legislated, policy makers would be powerless to act in the face of public demand for action. It should also be noted that those who control the "purse strings" would be very hesitant to abdicate that control to an automatic mechanism, especially with no proof that such a mechanism would work as proposed.

Despite the differences between Keynesianism and monetarists, they both rely on the fundamental fact that in both models, money effects NNP in the same way. In both theories, increasing the money supply will increase NNP. The debate centers around the amount, or weight, of change in NNP brought on by changes in the money supply. The major influence of the monetarist views has been to make policy makers more aware of the possibility of the crowding-out effect. In order to combat this possibility, changes in fiscal policy are now accompanied by consideration of changes in monetary policy. Using the tools together, changes in fiscal policy have less of a crowding-out effect if done simultaneously with changes in monetary policy. This is meant to ensure that the desired stimulating effect is not offset by contradictory forces.

As these debates went on in the 1960's, the American economy was doing well. There was great confidence in economists and the policy decisions being made. In the 1970's and into the early 1980's, things changed dramatically in ways that could not be explained, nor cured, by the current economic theories. The American economy was faced with the worst possible scenario: the stagnation of output and employment coupled with inflation. It was called, "stagflation".

The inability of economists and policy makers to explain it, let alone resolve it, shook the public's confidence in economists and in their theories. This gave rise to a new debate and a new theory called, "Supply-Side Economics."

On its face, Suppy-Side Economics appears to be a repackaging classical economic theory and a refinement of the monetarist's view. The difference was a focus on forces that adversely affected the "price" (P, or cost) component of the Equation of Exchange. Supply-Side economists felt Keynesian theory had been weakened because it had to be altered in an attempt to explain stagflation.

Using the Equation of Exchange (MV=PQ) it was theorizes! that during a severe recession, an increase in aggregate demand (MV) should have the effect of increasing output (Q) and reducing the unemployment rate. That would increase real output (Q) until full employment was reached. The price level (P) should have been constant until full employment was reached. ("Full employment" in this context, due to many factors, actually means about a 4% unemployment level, or near-full employment.) However, that was not what was happening. Under earlier theories, inflation would come about only if aggregate demand rose above what was required for full-employment, which would then cause prices to rise. This demand would pull inflation up. "Demand-Pull inflation" was widely accepted as being accurate.

Even with high unemployment during the 70's and 80's, inflation was a huge problem. There were increases in prices long before full-employment was achieved and Keynesian economics failed to explain it. It was than that work done by A.W. Phillips in the 1950's and 1960's came to the fore. He studied the relationship between the rate of unemployment and the rate of inflation. Based on this work, his explanation was adopted and called, the "Phillips Curve." (The Relationship between unemployment and the Rata of Change in Money Wage Rates in the United Kingdom, 1362-19 57, Economica, November, 1958, pp. 283-299.)

When the Phillips curve was applied to the data from the United States in the 1960's, it revealed that there was a direct correlation between the rate of unemployment and rising interest rates. There seemed to be a trade-off between employment and the price level. In order to achieve near-full-employment, society must endure higher inflation. However, to achieve price stability, the unemployment level must be at 6-7%. This showed that the theory of demand-pull inflation was incomplete, or too simplistic.

To explain this unfortunate correlation between the employment level and inflation, economists pointed to two factors. The first factor was said to be that there were imbalances, or bottlenecks, in the labor market as an economy expanded. The individual labor markets in the United States are segregated by occupation and geography. In fact, there are many different stratifications within the total labor force. These distinctions and differences meant that even as the economy expands, it will not effect the different labor pools equally. There will be shortages of labor and rising wages in some fields; while in other occupations, there will be no demand for labor. In the '70's and 80's, this was evident in that "professionals" and highly skilled workers had a very low unemployment rate while "unskilled" laborers had a very high unemployment rate. There were also vast differences by geographic region. People were simply unaware of job opportunities in other areas.

The conclusion was, although the overall unemployment rate was around 5 or 6%, there was a scarcity for labor in some professions and in some regions, but high unemployment in others. An expanding economy does not effect the labor force equally. The scarcity in some areas (both occupationally and geographically) meant higher wages for those labor pools. The increase in wages led to higher production costs and an increase in prices for all, even as the unemployment rate remained high.

Unfortunately, the idle labor pools did not have the agility, or wherewithal, to retrain rapidly enough to meet the needs of producers who were hiring. Retraining required money and time. By the time a worker retrained to work in another field, the opportunity may have passed. Plus, the worker may not have had the resources to survive while retraining. Such a venture was very risky. The unskilled remained unskilled and unemployed, even as prices were rising. Adding in factors such as discrimination, union restrictions, licensing requirements, and lack of knowledge about labor needs in other geographic areas; the structural dilemma concerning the different labor pools' inability to adapt was not easily resolved. Hence, the bottlenecks continued, and it continues to this day.

The second reason given to explain the Phillips Curve was that big businesses and labor unions had almost a monopoly power that allowed them to raise prices and demand higher wages. These demands are easier to exact as the economy nears full-employment. Economists deemed this "wage-push" or "cost-push" inflation. For example, if the economy is expanding and unions demand wage increases, businesses would be hesitant to forgo profits and face a costly strike. Instead, assuming they had near-monopoly power, they would grant the wage increases and simply pass on the higher production cost to the consumer. Along these same lines, with monopoly-like power, there can also be "profit-push" inflation where businesses can raise prices simply to increase their profit margin.

The possibility of wage-push, cost-push and/or profit-push inflation altered the theoretical economic outlook. It showed that the models of aggregate demand were insufficient and failed to explain stagflation without alteration. It was argued by the supply-side economists that fiscal and monetary policy adjustments simply moved the economy along the Phillips Curve and did not correct market imbalances. Because of the imbalances and other inflationary factors, fiscal and monetary policy could not sustain a simultaneous full-employment/stable price environment. To achieve those goals required breaking or shifting the Phillips Curve.

In order to counteract the imbalances in labor and the additional inflationary elements, several market policies were implemented. Also, pro-competitive legislation was enacted. The market policies put in place include vocational training, more job information and policies against discrimination. The pro-competitive policies were to reduce the monopoly power of businesses and unions through enforcement of anti-trust laws.

Unable to gain support or show the effectiveness of breaking up monopolies, there was then an attempt to constrain prices, wages and income through "guideposts". From 1962 to 1956, the Kennedy and Johnson administrations attempted to shift the Phillips Curve by establishing guideposts for "non-inflationary wage and price behavior." (Economic Report of the President, 1952 (Washington) pp. 185-190.) The wage guidepost was that wages in all industries should rise in accordance with the increased rate in labor productivity as a whole. The price guidepost was that prices should change to compensate for changes in labor costs.

Although irrelevant during the 1960's due to the Vietnam War, these guideposts were continued by President Nixon and enforced by law until 1974. President Carter attempted to bring these controls back in the late 1970's. It was not legislated, but pushed on the private sector as doing the socially responsible thing. These attempts to shift the Phillips Curve were untenable simply because across-the-board wage hikes and price increases led to misallocation of resources. This created inefficiencies that did the economy more harm than good.

Keynesian economists attempted to explain the failure of their model by pointing to unforeseen, abnormal circumstances. There was a shortage of agricultural products worldwide, which led to an explosion of food exports from the United States that led to higher domestic costs. There were shortages of certain raw materials. From 1971 to 1973, the dollar was devalued to help ease the United States' balance of payment deficits. But, economists cited the most important factor as being the four-fold increase in oil prices imposed by OPEC. All combined, Keynesians argued, the result was a boost in prices. The cost-side increases in prices reduced the amount of money consumers and investors had to spend.

The conclusion reached was that higher prices led to unemployment. For this reason, fiscal and monetary policy were ineffective in curing stagflation. This understanding opened the door for Supply-Side economics to take hold.

Supply-Siders called attention to fundamental changes in the economy that contributed to the worsening of the Phillips Curve. Their focus turned to what they felt were the biggest drags on the economy, the growth of the pubic sector and the high taxes needed to sustain such a large, intrusive government. They noted that the nation's tax bill was growing both in absolute terms and as a percentage of Gross National Product. Supply-side economists believed that the tax burden was having the same impact in shifting the Phillips Curve as other price increases had. They reasoned that the high level of taxes drove a "wedge" between the actual production cost of good and what consumers paid for those goods because businesses passed on the tax expenses onto consumers. The net effect of higher prices was higher unemployment.

The supply-side economists claimed that Keynesian economics did not come to terms with stagflation because the focus was on aggregate demand. Keynes had written against the backdrop of the Great Depression and focused on the problems of unemployment and excess capacity. This, the supply-siders said, was a whole new world. In addition, the tax-transfer system advocated by Keynesians, they felt, eroded the productivity of the economy and the decline in efficiency resulted in higher production costs and stagflation. The impact of taxes on a workers to pay for public programs meant less after-tax income or profits and that reduced the incentive to work hard.

Not surprisingly, the supply-side economists carried this further, adding that anything that added to the cost of production would increase inflationary pressures and cause unemployment. They pointed to government intervention and regulation as sources that contributed to the pricing "wedge". Specifically, they pointed to over-regulation in areas such as transportation and communication; and social regulation such as environmental controls, product safety, worker safety and equal opportuntity. To say that supply-side economists were of the conservative bent, i.e., pro-business, concerned mainly about the wealthiest individuals, would be an understatement. Things such as social good and more equal distribution of income were not just an onerous burdens, but an anathema.

The supply-side economist's proposed solution to stagflation was enacting massive tax-cuts and reduced government regulation. The posited that lower taxes would lead to a direct reduction in the tax wedge, increase productivity and the efficiency gains would result in lower costs of production per unit of output. In other words, drastic tax cuts, they believed, would shift the Phillips Curve in the direction they wanted.

At the time, Keynesian economists argued that reducing taxes so much would lead to very large budget deficits and accelerate the rate of inflation. Countering this assertion was Arthur Laffer, a supply-side economist at the University of Southern California. He put forth the idea that lower tax rates would actually increase tax revenue, and would not lead to inflationary deficits. His position was depicted in what is now called the Laffer Curve, which shows the relationship between tax rates and tax revenue. The basic idea is that there is a midpoint where maximum tax revue is obtained. His theory was that the higher tax rates discourage economic activity and reduce the tax base. Also, high taxes compelled people to find ways to avoid paying taxes. The higher the tax rate, the more tax evasion. At lower rates, i.e., the point where tax revenue is maximized, the risk of not paying taxes would be higher than simply paying what is owed. Also, the lower tax rate would tend to increase the incentives to work, save and invest, thus increasing the tax base. The expansion in national output and enlarged tax base would increase revenues enough to offset the loss from lower tax rates.

Realistically, it was easy to pick apart these assumptions. First, although no one could disagree with the proposition that at some point between 0 and 100%, there was an optimum level of taxation that would maximize revenue, but no one knew or could determine where on the Laffer Curve the economy was at that moment. If already situated below the optimum point, reducing taxes would reduce tax revenue. Second, there was no proof that people do not work, or they were less productive, because of higher taxes. That was just a supposition based on something that was impossible to measure. A worker could just as easily be less productive and work less because he was making more after-tax income.

The election of Ronald Reagan put the force of the Federal Government behind the theories and policies recommended by supply-side economists. In what was deemed, "trickle down economics" at the behest of the Republican Administration, there were across-the-board tax cuts. As nominal growth returned and inflation subsided, to the public, the supply-side economic policies had worked. However, a closer evaluation of that era reveals a different story. Prior to enacting the tax cuts, the Federal Reserve, during the Carter Administration, hiked up interest rates to unheard of levels in order to dampen inflation. For example, home mortgage rates were at 17%. After this tightening was done the data shows that the economy was beginning to recover, with tamer inflation, prior to Reagan taking office. As predicted and expected, there was a time lag between policy and results.

Secondly, during the eight years Reagan was in office, after the tax cuts, the national debt increased 180%. There was an increase in tax revenue and greater economic activity, but to say that was a result of the tax cuts or from massive government spending is not known. At the same time, the price of oil was cut by 1/3, and with the decline of influence from the Soviet Union (and eventual collapse), other economies experienced rapid expansion. In America, consumer's attitude started to change and they let go of the expectations of higher inflation. To say that the supply-side recommended tax cuts was the medicine that cured stagflation is a very simplistic view of reality. In the end, it was a complex combination of factors.

It is important to note that in the many years since, the "trickle down" theory of economics has not worked. As reported by many sources, real wages for laborers has not increased. The very wealthy now control a greater percentage of the world's assets than ever before; as the Bush tax cuts enacted from 2000 to 2008 had the effect of concentrating wealth even more. The disparity between the super-wealthy (the top 2% of earners) and the middle class has never been greater. In addition, the deregulation of the financial industry resulted in the catastrophic failure of industry titans, which required massive capital injections to keep banks solvent. After George Bush's supply-side economic policies, the United States was on the brink of another Great Depression. Since then, the focus has been on finding a path to economic stability.

Supply-side economics, despite the poor track record (massive national debt, housing bubble, credit crunch, financial collapse, more Americans living below the poverty line, stagnant real wage growth) has contributed to economic thought. The influence has been noted by policy makers playing closer attention to cost considerations that impact the economy as a whole. Economists of all persuasion now include supply, side analysis when evaluating policy decisions. While most economists take the position that the demand-side affect of tax cuts has a greater impact on NNP than it does on the supply side, using supply-side analyses can help explain subtleties Keynesian economic theory does not fully measure.

No matter the economic theory espoused, nor the political persuasion of the party in power, methods to remedy, predict and plan for various economic situations will continue to be debated. Because policy decisions are discretionary, how society reacts to the changing economic environment is an important element to gauge. Through the Rational Expectations Theory, there is the long-recognized view that any theory's predicted outcome depends upon what it assumes about expectations. There are three assumptions in the Rational Expectation Theory: 1) That individuals and businesses learn through experience to anticipate the consequences of changes in monetary and fiscal policy; 2) That individuals and businesses act instantaneously to protect their economic interests; and, 3) That all resources and product markets are purely competitive.

In the first assumption, that people and businesses learn through experience to anticipate the effects of changes in monetary and fiscal policy; not enough people are aware of or know how to react to changes in fiscal or monetary policy to make this a valid assumption. For those who are aware, namely the people and businesses for whom these decisions have the most impact, they attempt to adapt in anticipation. Following historical patterns, or what the "experts" tell them, they attempt to profit from policy changes, or shield their wealth.

For example, when the Federal Reserve announces interest rate cuts, the stock market usually rallies. Past indicators point to faster growth and higher corporate profits so people invest more. Even though past performance has not guaranteed that the stock market will rise, the expectation is that it will and the volume of buying on Wall Street sees a temporary upward swing. Whether or not those initial gains are sustained depends on how long after the policy change one examines.

Because there are few actions to be taken by the public in anticipation of fiscal policy changes, most people do not have any expectations and do nothing. Most people do not delay buying a house in anticipation of lower interest rates, nor do they sell based upon anticipated changes in tax policy. Most government spending has nothing to do with the majority of the public on an individual basis, so they do not act at all. The public seems more reactionary and only if something effects them directly, such as higher tax bills, will they take steps to ameliorate the potential loss of income.

Businesses and those who work in the financial sector may take a different approach. Based on prior experience, and because they have the financial resources to adjust, they may act in order to take advantage of anticipated changes in policy. It can be a sure bet that in a recession, prior to a decision on interest rates, where a cut is expected, financial firms will commit more funds into riskier assets in anticipation of a rapid increase in the stock indices. Getting in the market before the masses and getting out soon after the initial surge reduces the return to private investors, but that does not frustrate the attempts of policy makers to increase economic activity. Or, in anticipation of large quantities of Treasury bond sales by the Federal Reserve, which would reduce their value, firms may sell their Treasury holdings before the auction. The effect of this would be to increase the yield demanded by investors, increasing interest rates, thereby magnifying what may be the Fed's attempt to tighten the money supply.

A massive spending bill passed by Congress in 2009, with the hundreds of billions of dollars of stimulus, what could a private citizen do in anticipation of its passage? Most of the money is earmarked for public works, unavailable to private citizens, and has little to no impact on their lives. Even a contractor in the business of delivering concrete, who may hope to capitalize on the stimulus bill, could do nothing that would counteract the intended effects of the spending. Acting in his own best interest, in anticipation of a big contract, he may "lock-in" prices on raw materials before they rise as demand increases. But, that would have a positive, stimulating effect as his order would create demand, and that would be the direction the spending bill intends.

For those who have the capacity to act, they do and will act in their own self-interest. Whether that has the ability to frustrate the actions of policy makers is questionable. In the aggregate, the response of society and business firms in expectation of policy changes would not be enough to offset or frustrate the intent of the policy makers. There are several reason why responses by the public would not render discretionary policies ineffective. A small segment of the population, in anticipation, and for their own economic self-interest, would attempt to act, but would do the wrong thing. Despite claims to the contrary, there are many individuals who do not act rationally. In the past ten years, there have been several examples of millions of people acting irrationally, although they believed they were doing the right thing. Recently, the demand by individuals to hold the commodity gold has increased as people expect the value of the dollar to decline. Whether holding a non-interest bearing commodity that is less liquid and subject to wild price swings may or may not be the right move. But, that in no way becomes a detriment to the enacted fiscal and monetary policies.

Another large segment of the population does not have the financial resources to do anything at all, and even if they did, would not know what to do. Finally, the vast majority of society does not pay attention to policy changes at all, let alone act to anticipate them. These conditions seem to indicate there is little to no effect in anticipation to policy changes. The question becomes if the small sliver of the population who can act in anticipation has enough economic force to frustrate policy.

However, there are hedge funds, financial firms, who do nothing but speculate, using massive amounts of money, coupled with leverage, in order to capitalize on changes in monetary and fiscal policy. These firms do have the ability through flash trading to buy and sell derivatives in seconds, and make profits doing such trades. If there is a source of frustration concerning the Rational Expectations Theory, it is from the hedge funds.

In this recession, with high unemployment, the anticipation of loose monetary policy that will eventually lead to inflation, did not compel workers to demand higher wages. Instead, the public is so afraid of losing what jobs they do have, they have been accepting pay cuts and reduced hours. It is a complete fallacy to think that individuals react in anticipation of future inflation due to an increase in the money supply. Instead, they are worried about paying their bills now and putting food on the table.

Even the middle class, due to their choice in lifestyle, lives paycheck to paycheck. This is evidenced by the housing bubble and record number of mortgage foreclosures.

To say that individuals act instantaneously to protect their own economic interests would be true if they had the means to act, the knowledge of what to do, and the awareness to know there there is a pending policy change. There seems to be two different worlds separated by wealth. If policy makers believe that the vast majority of the public is anything more than powerless to benefit from anticipated change in fiscal policy, it is because they live in the world of the wealthy and are out of touch with reality.

To complete the picture, the question remains whether businesses, who do have the means and knowledge to act instantaneously to protect their economic interests actually do so. It appears they would, but not to the extent that would put their business at risk. A major aspect of modern business concerns risk management. Aware that policy decisions sometimes have unintended consequences, and because firms use long-term contracts to hedge against inflation, there would seem to be little room to maneuver for the more conservative businesses.

The final issue is if all resources and product markets are purely competitive. The answer to that is a resounding, "no". There is no such thing as a purely competitive market. The closest thing to a purely competitive market can be found in agriculture. Class I corn is Class I corn, there are many producers, and no distinction between corn produced from those producers. However, there can be slight variations, based on the method of farming, whether it is organic or inorganic, whether the seeds have been genetically altered or not. Suddenly, price difference appear, even though corn is still corn.

Due to changes in transportation and communication, along with lower barriers to trade, most markets are competitive, but not purely. Through mergers and acquisitions, and because of high barriers to entry, it seems that most markets have coalesced into oligopolies. Because of costs, legal restrictions, and regulation, there does seem to be a barrier to entry in many markets. Add in international trade and it becomes more difficult to establish a profitable business in any market. To compete and be profitable, the direction has been towards consolidation to take advantage of economies of scale and improve efficiency.

It is important to note that the economy of the United States is more dependent upon international trade than ever, with multinational corporations dominating economic activity.

Therefore, policy decisions, be it fiscal or monetary, do not just effect the United States, but the ripples are felt worldwide. As entire nations engage in trade, effecting prices and either adding stability or instability to commodity prices, economic theory has become a lot more complicated.

John Maynard Keynes and Milton Friedman both contributed greatly to economic thought. Their research and theories changed the way people thought about money. Based upon their explainations and policies dictated by their theories, it can be argued that they have helped this nation pull out of the Great Depression and eventually beat stagflation. Mo one could know what would have happened if the United States Government would have retained its laissez faire stance on economic policy.

In the years since the creation of the Federal Reserve and the Employment Act of 1946, the environment has improved for the American worker. Households have experienced an increased standard of living and though there have been periods of economic turmoil, alterations and refinements of economic models have helped explain them, and set courses for action to avert financial disasters.

The world has changed since Keynes articulated his theories and Friedman added his refienments. Economists are aware that policy makers cannot easily predict the outcome of policy changes, nor can they predict every eventuality. Also, no matter the school of thought, even supply-side economists, it is well recognized that it takes a combination of actions to change the economic landscape because many elements and factors are interdependent.

Based on recent experiences and outcomes from fiscal policy, it seems clear that the problems articulated by Keynes still exist. The price system has led to economic instability, misallocation of resources and income inequalities. Milton Friedman was also correct in that some attempts to remedy these shortcomings through fiscal policy is ineffective, but his arguments that stability could only come about through automatic increases in the money supply fell flat. The shortcoming of the Equation of Exchange is in the simplistic view that the velocity of money in a constant.

The Keynesian view of the money supply was that changes in monetary policy were inefficient, requiring a long chain of events before an increase would effect NNP. Even then, the results would be uncertain. It was for this reason, Keynesians put less emphasis on monetary policy and more on fiscal policy.

Friedman's had a negative view of manipulating the economy through fiscal policy. He, and the monetarists, felt that fiscal policy undermined stability, was wasteful and added to socio-economic ills. Monetarists believed that the price system was more efficient and put a much greater value in adding the money supply in order to provide stabilized growth.

The monetarist's views were refined, repackaged and expanded upon by supply-side economists. Supply-side economists used the inability of the Keynesian theory of employment to explain stagflation as an opening to expanded the debate. Factoring in the supply-side of the economic equation led to more policy changes that greatly reduced taxes and regulation in an attempt to achieve stable growth and full employment. Policy makers became more conscious of the effects of monetary and fiscal policy changes on both the demand and supply side of the employment equation. To make policy changes more effective, they often consider fiscal and monetary policy changes together.

Facing the current economic crisis, a steep recession, massive national debt, severe budget deficits, the current debate centers around economic recovery. From the several schools of economic thought, the voice of Keynes and Friedman can still be heard. It is yet to be seen if the combination of increasing the money supply, as Friedman would advocate as the most efficient remedy, and massive government stimulus, as Keynes would have suggested as the proper solution, will work. Then, it is yet to be seen if the combination of policy actions will swing the economy into a period of rapidly rising inflation and how the Federal Reserve acts to shrink the money supply in order to stave off inflation.

Because the stimulus injected into the economy has no equal in historic terms, several economic theories can be tested and evaluated. The policy changes were not subtle, so the effect on NNP, income, prices, interest rates, employment, investment, savings and inflation should be evident. One theory, the Rational Expectations Theory, has already seemed to be proven wrong. Even after policy changes took effect, there was little reaction that would tend to negate or frustrate the intent of the policy changes. There is no evidence to suggest that the effect of discretionary changes in the money supply is muted by anticipatory reations.

There are factors now present in our economy that were unthinkable in the days of Keynes and Friedman. Changes in the world, changes in technology, transportation, communication and society as a whole. It will be interesting to sea if the American economy can adapt to the challenges, which school of economic though can better predict and find solutions to the troubles ahead. It can been argued that the United States is in a transitional phase with major implications on the economy as a whole. Questions remain whether consumer confidence will return and if that will lead to more spending and a higher velocity of money.

If the short-term trends continue, individuals will continue to live within their means, borrow less, save more and be more averse to risk. It may very well be that fear of economic collapse and instability from no job security will lead American consumers to act more rationally. That would mean a long-term change in the velocity of money, higher savings rates, lower interest rates and more stability. The question of how the government will cure its financial ills is yet to be resolved.

Founding Economics

"The ideas of economists and political philosophers, both when they are right and when they are wrong, are more powerful than is commonly understood. Indeed the world is ruled by little else. Practical men, who believe themselves to be quite exempt from any intellectual influences, are usually the slave of some defunct economist." John Maynard Keynes, quoted in The Age of the Economist, 3rd Ed., Daniel R. Fusfeld, 1977.

This Nation was founded upon the notion of self-determination. It was the onerous taxes and price controls implemented by the English Crown that compelled a revolution in America. The founding documents of this nation and the debates establishing our Government make it clear: what we as a people wanted was freedom. A cornerstone of freedom and self-determination is economic freedom. What was established by declaring independence and what is written in the Constitution is the foundation of freedom, including: the rule of law, limitations on government power and interference, property rights and limitations on taxation. All of these elements are economic and established the basis for a free market economy. Because of our system of what is primarily a capitalist economy, Americans were able to have their self-determination and prosper.

The early years of the United States was marked by erratic, unstable markets. There was little central planning and currencies from many nations were in use. In 1790, on the advice of the Secretary of Treasury, Alexander Hamilton, Congress created the First United States Bank. This was done in order to eliminate inefficiencies in the young Republic by creating a standard currency and a place where the government could deposit its funds. Also, a national bank would help in the collection of taxes and assist both the government and businesses by increasing the amount of capital necessary for expansion. The First United States Bank's charter was granted in 1791, but expired in 1811. After years of dissension from rural and Southern States, the Senate refused to grant a new charter.

At the same time, protectionist policies, first advocated by Hamilton and initiated in 1791, imposed tariffs on foreign goods. This allowed newly formed industries in the United States to grow. Again in 1816, large tariffs were levied against European goods as the British dumped low-cost merchandise into the American market in an attempt to squeeze American manufacturers out of business. The Government intervention into markets provided American producers the ability to survive adverse market conditions.

Without the stabilizing force of a national bank, the economy went into disarray. There were many "local" currencies with no control over how much was printed and no way to establish exchange rates. This had the effect of destabilizing the Nation. It was inefficient and inadequate. The Federal Government did not have a central planning agency. During the War of 1812, in order to finance the war, the Government was forced to sell bonds, bills and notes and institute direct taxes. Because of that experience, Congress chartered the Second Bank of the United States.

The prosperity of the people was dependent on the stability and reliability of the currency as a means of trade. Caught between the desire to limit the influence of the Federal Government and the need for a stable banking system, our political leaders chose a "hands-off" approach to banking. In 1836, the Charter of the Second United States Bank expired. Though the United States grew and prospered, it was not without economic turmoil. Because of rampant inflation, and exaggerated business cycles, booms and busts and panics caused havoc. There were wild swings in the national economy in 1819, 1837, 1857, 1873 and in 1907. These events brought great economic chaos and social misery to our nation.

It was clear, based on this history, that an unstable monetary system had exaggerated business cycles. A central control of monetary policy was necessary Under President Woodrow Wilson, in 1913, the Federal Reserve Act was passed. The creation of a central bank was a major step away from a "pure" free-market economy and towards a "mixed" market economy, with the Federal Government retaining some control over the economy and the major factors that control economic conditions.

The productivity of the American worker, combined with advances in technology, some spurred by war that required the advent of new manufacturing processes, and the specialization of vocations within industries and by geography -- along with massive amounts of natural resources, propelled the United States. By 1894, in terms of manufacturing output and the standard of living, the United States ranked first in the world.

Further Federal action was necessary to even the playing field and to reduce the power and influence of several monopolies in specific industries. Contrary to a pure capitalistic system, intervention through the Interstate Commerce Act (1887), The Sherman Anti-Trust Act of 1890 and the Clayton Act of 1914 empowered the Federal Government to break monopolies that had an adverse effect on the economy and consumers. Using these powers, the result was increased competition and reduced prices.

Having one currency, creating markets for commercial paper (short-term loans) and the ability to manipulate the amount of currency in circulation, gave the Federal Reserve System the ability to reign in business cycles. The creation of the Federal Deposit Insurance Corporation in 1935 gave Americans confidence in the banking system, that their savings were safe. Using the tools of interest rate manipulation and bond purchases or sales, the Government had in place what it needed to maintain growth and stability in the American economy. This was the dawn of the economist.

"Economics is concerned with the efficient utilization or management of limited resources for the purpose of attaining the maximum satisfaction of human material wants." Economics, Principles, Problems and Policies, Campbell McConnell, 1981.

At its core, economics is the study of human behavior; man's wants, needs and desires and how to provide them. It is the analysis of supply and demand; and the theories relating to exchanging, producing, and consuming material goods and services that people want and need. The quantitative and qualitative analysis of man's wants and needs, along with providing for those wants and needs, extends from each individual in their choices -- all the way out to governments -- and effects everything in between. Aware of it or not, everyone operates according to economic theory or is subject to conditions based upon economic policies. Simply stated, economics determines who gets what and for how much; because with limited resources, everyone cannot have everything they desire.

How do we use scare resources efficiently? How do we determine the most efficient way to distribute a limited amount of commodities? What method do we use to maximize the potential of hard earned dollars? What forces dictate how a government establishes tax policy for the benefit of its citizens? These issues, along with many others, are based on economics.

Economics is also the discipline of maximizing efficiencies in order to satisfy the needs of the most people. Stemming from the economic theories of Adam Smith, John Stewart Mill, David Ricardo, Karl Marx, and John Maynard Keyes, philosophically driven political divisions were created. Capitalism, Communism, and Socialism are all based upon divergent economic theory. That we live in a mixed-market economy with limited central control is based upon the choice of the people. Who we elect as our President and representatives dictates whether we strictly adhere to free market policies or adopt socialistic principles. At that level, economics is concerned with society as a whole.

At the business level, and at the individual level, economics is used to plan and forecast, to set price points at which to buy or sell goods and services, and to try and determine the best course or action given a variety of factors. At any level, one using the discipline of economics first establishes facts that are relevant to a problem. Then, one develops theories or principles that generalize about economic behavior. Based on those principles, one then initiates policies to try and reach the desired effect.

Macro-Economics/Micro-Economics

Since this discipline is based on facts, observable, verifiable behaviors, the principles and policies developed to find solutions to problems are only as sound as the accuracy of the facts they are based upon. As with all human endeavors, it is impossible to predict human behavior with 100% accuracy. Because of this, nothing is "for sure" in economics. That is why determinations and policies are based on generalizations.

There are variables that effect economics that cannot be known until they occur. The term "irrational exuberance" was used by Alan Greenspan to describe the stock market bubble in the late 1990's. People were not being rational and were paying large sums for shares in companies that never earned a dime. The market then was well beyond sustainable levels and fell when consumers regained realistic expectations.

An economist may come up with a theory based upon the latest statistical analysis of known facts, generate models that can be tested on the fastest super-computers using thousands of variables, and still predict the wrong outcome of a policy. Yet, through economics, a systematic approach is utilized to better understand what works to improve a situation and what does not. By necessity, economic principles are therefore an abstraction, because nothing is static.

Economics operates at two distinct levels, the macroeconomic level and the microeconomic level. Macroeconomic analysis is concerned with the economy as a whole or with primary subdivisions, or aggregates. Some examples of aggregates would be the Government, all households, or business sectors that make up the economy. These large segments comprise many individual units but are lumped together and treated as one unit. Macroeconomics is concerned with obtaining an overview, or general outline, of the structure of the economy and the relationship among the aggregates that make up the economy.

When speaking in macroeconomic terms, the small, individual units are not considered. Instead, topics relate to such things as total output, total level of employment or total expenditures -- all which relate to the aggregate. There is an attempt to achieve a sort of "omniscient" point of view of the economy as a whole.

Conversely, microeconomics is concerned with specific economic units and a very detailed consideration of the behavior of those individual units. Whatever is being analyzed at the microeconomic level is put under a figurative microscope and dissected so that the details of its operation can be observed. When speaking of things in microeconomic terms, everything is very specific, such as a particular business or a household and the focus is as detailed as the optimum price-point for a particular product. Microeconomics is useful to pinpoint minute efficiencies in very specific components of our economic system.

Topics such as the money supply, total bank deposits, and Government spending fall into the domain of macroeconomics. The monetary system is the lifeblood of an economy. The money supply is the total amount of money available in our system. Defining the money supply requires agreement as to what constitutes "money". The definition can be narrow, encompassing coins, paper money, and demand deposits -- while including savings accounts and some Government bonds is the broader definition. The overall money supply and its effect on the economy is analyzed through the lens of macroeconmics.

A primary example of macroeconomics is when the Federal Reserve acts to tamp down inflation or deal with a recession. Using economic theories, the Federal Reserve attempts to influence the rate of growth by either increasing or decreasing the total amount of money in the economy. Based on factual scenarios presented at the time, the Federal Reserve (the Fed) sets target growth rates and uses economic models in an attempt to achieve and maintain a stable growth rate. To do this, the Fed has several tools -- and, as of late, the Fed has been using them all in order to stimulate the economy by having a "loose" monetary policy and increasing the total amount of dollars in the monetary system.

The primary tool of the Fed is interest rates. When banks deposit funds with the Fed, the Fed pays them interest. In addition, the Fed sets the rate that banks pay to each other for short-term loans. By lowering the interest rate, there is less of an incentive (less profit potential for banks) to deposit funds into the Federal Reserve or to loan money to another bank. This then gives banks the incentive to loan the money to consumers or businesses in order to increase their profit potential. What interest rates banks charge consumers has a direct correlation to the Fed's manipulation of the rates they pay. For the consumer, more money available makes it easier to get loans and it costs them less. For these reasons, maintaining low target interest rates is termed "loose" monetary policy, because it is easier to obtain.

Conversely, when there is too much growth and inflation is a problem, the Fed raises the interest rates they pay banks, and the rates banks can charge each other. The effect of more money being put into reserve, where the banks earn a guaranteed rate of return, decreases the amount of money being loaned to consumers or businesses. The less money there is to loan, the harder it is to get a loan, the more expensive it is to borrow money, which results in less economic activity. Raising interest rates is called "tightening", because it is harder to get loans.

In addition to manipulating interest rates, the Federal Reserve can also increase or decrease the percentage of deposits member banks are required to hold in reserve. This is a function of the Federal Deposit Insurance Corporation, but the mandated percent of reserves is controlled by the Fed in order to manipulate the overall money supply.

Another device at the Federal Reserve's disposal is the buying and selling of Treasury bills, bonds and notes. The Federal Reserve holds trillions of dollars worth of these securities on their balance sheet. The Federal Government, through the United States Treasury, borrows money and the Federal Reserve buys some of the debt instruments (loans the money) and holds the securities. In times of inflation, to reduce the amount of money in the money supply, the Federal Reserve sells the Treasury bonds it holds to the public (individuals, firms, and foreign governments). The money they take in from the sale of the bonds has the effect of reducing the amount of money in the economy. During recessionary times, the Fed does the opposite -- they buy bonds from the public, paying out cash and increasing the money supply.

One tool of the Federal Reserve is commonly referred to as "printing money." Although the Fed does supply the actual currency in the form of "Federal Reserve Notes," at such a massive scale necessary to alter the money supply, the actual printing of paper bills plays only a small part. Instead, what the Fed does is purchase assets from banks or other financial institutions and credits the amount in that institution's reserve account. It is not a physical transfer of currency, although that does occur as needed to meet the physical demand for currency; the real action is an adjustment to an account balance. Whatever assets the Feds buys, whether it be billions of dollars worth of short-term notes, commercial paper, or mortgage backed securities, transfers to the Fed's balance sheet in return for the credit that is then added to the account of the seller. Having a higher balance in reserve allows banks to make more money available for loans. It is very rare that the Federal Reserve uses this method to increase the total money supply. It is considered a drastic action used in the most pressing times because it requires adding lower quality (riskier) assets to the Federal Reserve's balance sheet.

Because increases and decreases in the money supply using these tools have drastic effects, there is always the risk of providing too much stimulus, which would cause inflation, or pulling too much money out of the system, which would cause a recession. It is the domain of macroeconomics to try and predict the proper interest rates so that there is sustained, slow growth in the overall economy. This is no easy task since the economy is so massive and so dynamic.

"The difficult questions concerning paper [money] are . . . not about its economy, convenience or ready circulation but about the amount of paper that can be widely issued or created, and the possibilities of violent convulsions when it gets beyond bounds." F. W. Taussig, Principles of Economics, 4th ed, 1946.

The recent worldwide recession and attempts to stimulate the economy are a prime example of macroecomics at work. The stimulus coming from Government spending and actions of the Federal Reserve are meant to increase total employment and increase the gross national product. As more and more capital becomes available, it is intended to effect the nation's economy on a grand scale. However, the Fed already has plans to reduce the money supply when necessary, in order to stave off inflation, growth that is so rapid that prices rise too quickly and the value of the dollar decreases sharply. These plans are in place because there is a great risk the Government has gone too far or may maintain a "loose" monetary policy for too long.

What caused this current recession is something that requires further analysis. Depending on one's perspective, the reason for the current turmoil can vary from the prior administration's lax regulatory environment, to what has been deemed a "housing bubble" that crashed. However, in macroeconomic terms, many of the oft stated reasons are overly simplistic. How to prevent the same type of crisis in the future will require more study and a deeper understanding. In addition, the proper tools must be in place to make the economic cycles less severe. The macroeconomists are the ones who are trying to understand what happened, why and what to do about it. They are also the ones who will try and figure out what can be done so the same events do not happen in the future.

In order to show microeconomics at work, the focus must narrow from the broad total economy to an individual firm and an individual consumer. The following examples illustrate how one can use microeconomic theories to maximize profits for the business and how a consumer maximizes his or her satisfaction.

Illustrating a company's desire to maximize profits for a particular product requires factual determinations which can be charted and plotted against the expected behavior of the consumer. Several assumptions must be made. First, it is assumed that the business is one with lots of competition. In other words, it does not maintain a monopoly in the market nor is there one dominant firm capable of altering the market price. Second, there must be an assumption that the product is similar, but not identical to, other products being sold by other firms (either through material differences or advertising). Additionally, the large volumes of product being produced by all firms combined with the uniqueness of the products makes the demand for the firm's product conform with the market demand. Finally, there is an assumption that there is some barrier to entry, so that new firms cannot suddenly jump into the market and add additional supply. This assumptions allow for the application of "the theory of the firm."

The theory of the firm explains how businesses determine what level of production they should maintain in order to obtain maximum profits. Under ordinary circumstances, as the output of any product increases beyond a certain volume, its costs conform to the law of diminishing returns. This theory is based on the knowledge that as output increases, fixed costs are spread over more units sold, thus initially reducing the average cost per unit. However, as output increases further, eventually the law of diminishing returns exerts influence, causing variable costs to rise.

In order to determine the exact level of output for maximum profit potential, a firm must determine their fixed costs, items they must pay regardless of total production. These items include: principal and interest on loans, rent, taxes and contract wages. Then, they must determine the variable costs according to the volume of production. These include cost of labor, raw materials, distribution, plant maintenance and utilities. As stated, the variable costs decline per unit at the early stages of production but increase beyond the point of diminishing returns. For example, if an overtime shift is required to increase the volume of units produced, that would necessitate paying overtime and would raise the variable production cost per unit.

Applying these calculations, the firm determines the average cost of production per unit by adding the fixed cost per unit to the variable cost per unit at set production levels. If plotted on a graph, initially, with each additional unit, the average cost of production would decline. Eventually the cost of production will start to rise. It would not be a straight line, but a curved line.

In order to find the solution, it is a necessity for the firm to accurately gauge the anticipated revenue in order to maximize profits. The firm could not sell the product above the established market price of similar products without losing customers. Using that price point, the average revenue per unit can be determined.

Profit is calculated by subtracting the total cost of production from the revenue received. Once the average revenue per product is compared to, or plotted against, the average cost per product at each production level, maximum profit potential can be easily deduced. Where revenue exceeds cost by the greatest amount, profits are maximized.

Using microeconomics to determine how consumers maximize their satisfaction also requires several assumptions. The primary assumption is that a consumer acts rationally. The consumer attempts to dispose of his or her money so as to obtain the maximum usefulness or utility from their money. In other words, the rational consumer wants to get the most for their money. The second assumption is that the consumer has clear-cut preferences in the market of the products they select. In addition, the consumer is aware that at some point the utility of the product diminishes as they accumulate a larger amount.

Budget Example

Finally, it is assumed that the consumer has a limited amount of income, requiring a budget and the inability to buy indiscriminately.

"In making his choices, our typical consumer is in the same position as the Western prospector who is restocking for his next trip into the back country and who is forced by the nature of the terrain to restrict his luggage to whatever he can carry on his back or burro. If he takes a great deal of one item, say baked beans, he must necessarily take much less of something else, say bacon. His job is to find the collection of products which, in view of the limitations imposed on the total, will best suit his needs and taste." E. T. Weiler, The Economic System, 1952.

In determining a consumer's maximum satisfaction, one must employ the utility maximizing rule which states: "The consumer's money should be allocated so that the last dollar spent on each product purchased yields the same amount or extra (marginal) utility." Economics, Principles, Problems and Policies, Campbell McConnell, 1981. Also, it is necessary to understand the law of diminishing marginal utility. "Utility" is defined as "want satisfying power." (Id.) In other words, "utility" does not just mean "useful" but it can also mean the power to satisfy wants. A bottle of Pepsi may not be useful, but it is satisfying to a consumer and meets their needs. Once the meaning of utility is understood, the law of diminishing marginal utility can be put into context.

Someone who does not own a computer but needs one has a strong desire to obtain one. Once they have a computer, the need and desire for a second computer is reduced. A third computer may be all but useless and there is probably no desire or need to have four or more computers under normal circumstances. In other words, "marginal utility" means the extra satisfaction a consumer gets from one additional unit of a specific product. The law of diminishing utility is that the "marginal utility derived from successive units of a given product will decline." (Id.) Clearly, this must take place over a very short amount of time and in that time, the consumer's taste does not change.

It is the consumer who must make the choices. This makes the evaluation of a consumer's satisfaction completely subjective. Of all of the collections of goods and services which a consumer can obtain within his or her means, which specific combination will yield the most satisfaction? To simplify this analysis, it is necessary to limit the discussion to a few products and one small purchase. It then necessary to assess a consumer's attitude and preferences, along with the utility (derived satisfaction) from what they are going to purchase. Once a consumer weighs their preferences, the income available, and the price of other goods, a determination can be made that reveals the maximum satisfaction.

Assume a consumer wanted to purchase a combination of two different products with a set amount of dollars. Product "A" offers twice as much satisfaction but costs twice as much as the second product, Product "B". However, the more of each product he or she buys of each, the less useful or satisfying it is. At some point, it would simply be a waste to buy any more -- a saturation point. Assuming the consumer spends all of the money they have allocated, say, $10, it can be determined how many of each product they should buy to achieve maximum satisfaction.

What has to be determined is the level of satisfaction per dollar spent on each product and the rate of diminishing usefulness of each product with each additional purchase. Once the subjective variables are known, such as the satisfaction or marginal utility of each unit of a product, and it is quantified, and a saturation point is known, the solution to the problem is found by determining the maximum marginal utility up to the last dollar spent. This solution also corresponds to and can be expressed using a demand curve.

In the example charted below, buying three units of product "A" and four units of product "B" achieves maximum satisfaction. This number is reached by summing up the satisfaction derived at each level of units purchased and adding that to the sum of the satisfaction level of units of the second product at the proper ratio.

	PRODUCT "A"—$2.00			PRODUCT B-- $1.00	
	MARGINAL	MARGINAL		MARGINAL	MARGINAL
UNIT	UTILITY/ UNIT	UTILITY/ DOLLAR	UNIT	UTILITY/ UNIT	UTILITY/ DOLLAR
1st	12	6	1st	6	6
2nd	10	5	2nd	5	5
3rd	8	4	3rd	4	4
4th	6	3	4th	3	3
5th	4	2	5th	2	2
			6th	1	1
			7th	0	0
TOTAL TO SPEND=		$10	8th	0	0
			9th	0	0
			10th	0	0

TOTAL MARGINAL

UNITS F   UNITS OF B   UTILITY
OF A

UNITS OF A	UNITS OF B	TOTAL MARGINAL UTILITY
5	0	20
4	2	29
3	4	33 (highest satisfaction)
2	6	32
1	8	27
0	10	21

In this example, the first unit of product "A" has a marginal utility per dollar spent of 6. The second unit purchased has a marginal utility of 5, the third, 4, but the total marginal utility derived by purchasing three units of product "A" is 15 per dollar (6 + 5 + 4). Having spent only $6, four units of product "B" can be bought, with a total marginal utility of 18 (6+5+4+3). Adding 15 to 18 gives us 33. Using this method, an equilibrium is achieved and the maximum level of satisfaction is pinpointed.

An alternative method can be used to answer this question. One could determine all possible combinations of the number of units that can be purchased given the prices of each item and the amount of money allocated to make the purchase. Instead of applying a subjective rating to each product at each increased unit of purchase (applying the diminished marginal utility factor) the consumer could simply choose based upon the satisfaction level at each ratio of product "A" to product "B".

The solution is still dependent on the consumer's satisfaction levels and it is valid unless he or she is indifferent to the ratio of the first product to the second. Determining the proper ratio is thus simply a function of choosing the combination with the highest utility to the consumer. The simplicity of this method is that the consumer only has to specify whether a given combination of product "A" and product "B" meets their needs, or has more utility than any other combination -- as opposed to attempting to numerically quantify the utility and diminishing marginal utility rate of both products. Simply put, how many $1 bags of chips and how many $2 bottles of soda do they want to buy with $10. The proper choice is whatever ratio meets their needs.

Using microeconomics, it is not possible to perfectly predict the behavior of consumers or determine a perfect price point to maximize profit potential. However, using models and generalizations that have a close correlation to reality makes it possible to narrow the margin of error and achieve greater efficiencies.

Economics, on its own, is not meant as an exact science that generates products and profits. Instead, it provides people, business and Governments with methods to find solutions to problems. As far back in history as one looks, we can see economic principles at work. From the times of Feudalism, where land owners devised methods to determine how to best allocate their property, to cavemen deciding to cultivate land instead of constantly roaming and chasing game to survive. These were decisions based on economics. Even though things like "economy of scale" and "maximizing efficiency" were not defined terms, they were still acted upon, because they were intuitive. The actions taken lead to greater satisfaction, and increased the possibility of survival.

Intuition is still part of the discipline of economics. No matter where an economist studied or how terrific their computer software is, if they include false assumptions or make generalizations that do not correspond to reality or how markets behave, solutions cannot be found. Economics does require many sets of skills, but nothing is more important that understanding human behavior -- because what economics comes down to at the macro and micro levels is meeting the needs of people.

"Like all scientific laws, economic laws are established in order to make successful prediction of the outcome of human actions." Oskar Lange, "The Scope and Method of Economics," Reviews of Economic Studies, vol. 13, 1945-46, p.20.

ECONOMICS, SCARCITY, SOCIETY AND PRODUCTION

The central facts of economics are that society's material wants are virtually unlimited, or insatiable, and that economic resources are limited, or scarce. Everything in the realm of economics is either directly or indirectly dependent upon these facts. Unlimited wants juxtaposed against limited resources create situations that determine prices, levels of satisfaction, and the availability or scarcity of goods and services. From the counter-opposing forces of supply and demand, factors such as wages effect us at the individual level. Government intervention into markets effects society as a whole. Through economic theory, policies and practices are determined and put into place in attempts to maximize efficiencies, increase productivity and potentially satisfy as many people as possible using the several means of production. The global economy is an organic system, constantly growing and changing and no matter the philosophy, the core facts of economics -- insatiable wants and scarce resources -- still holds true. Finding the maximum benefit for all requires that diverse economic systems work together.

The first fact fundamental to economics is that society, people and institutions, have unlimited material wants. "Material wants" signifies the desire of the consumer to obtain various goods and utilize various services. These goods and services give the consumer pleasure or satisfaction, or fulfill a need. The list of possible goods and services is seemingly endless: food, clothes, housing, and medical services are just a few examples of necesscities. There are also luxuries such as gold and diamond jewelry, that also satisfy human wants. Add in the different varieties of products and levels of quality of these necessities and luxuries, and the array of products and services in demand is vast.

What products are made available, with what distinctive features and in what supply depends on demand. It is true that "higher quality" or "better" in relation to particular goods and services can be a subjective measure in some instances. However, the diversity in products creates deamand and provides choices. Along with the forces of competition and the level of output, prices are set. These factors help propel the economic cycle.

In addition, what one might deem a luxury, another may see as a necessity. The main point is that all of the goods and services are capable of satisfying a human want. Services can be as satisfying as material goods in that they have an equal capacity to meet a need. Someone who needs their car to get to work finds the service of the mechanic who can fix his car very valuable. The cab driver taking him to work as he waits for his car to be fixed has provided a valuable service that has met his needs.

Businesses and governments also have wants and needs and vie for the same limited resources. Land, labor, buildings, machinery, and raw materials are sought after by businesses. Governments, in order to meet the needs of the people, obtain property for schools and highways, allocate resources to buy construction materials and procure military hardware to protect the citizens.

The term, "insatiable" in the context of all consumers must be properly understood. The need for goods and services is constantly changing according to a variety of factors. For example, in the 1970's, there was only a very small demand for computers limited to businesses, institutions and governments. Today, computers are cheap, easy to use and ubiquitous. Almost everyone uses them, has them, and wants them in one form or another. Buying a new computer may satisfy a need, but only temporarily. Sooner or later, it will break down, or new products will be introduced with better features. The want for a new computer will then re-emerge. A person may buy a Ford, but they are still tempted by the Porsche, and if they had the funds to buy it, they would. Some needs are temporarily met, but, there will always be a demand for more or better. Needs and wants in general, are never completely satisfied.

Another feature of human wants and needs is that they vary over time. A particular product may satisfy them one day but may not satisfy them the next. Someone with massive resources could completely satisfy a particular need or want, but other needs or wants would arise. After buying her tenth car, a billionaire might not be interested in cars any longer, but her attention may turn to yachts, or houses. We cannot get enough goods and services.

Some of the wants are a function of technological advances with new products and new product cycles. Some of the desire for material goods is a function of advertising or peer pressure. In other instances, wants and needs are dictated by society, or by the culture we live in. Whether deemed a luxury or necessity, the demand for goods and services multiplies and changes over time, creating a never-ending cycle. Whatever the case, humans are almost never satisfied with what they have and the objective of all economic activity is the attempt to satisfy the diverse material wants and needs.

It is also a fact that economic resources are scarce. There is a limit to everything and it would be impossible to produce enough goods and provide all of the service everyone wanted. "Economic resources" means all of the natural resources, all of the human resources, and all of the manufactured resources that go into the production of goods or utilization of services.

There is only so much arable land for farming or to plant trees. There is only so much gold and oil in the world. It can be difficult and expensive to get to these resources, refine them, and bring to market. Only so many machines used to produce goods can be made; and they eventually break down, become obsolete and need to be replaced. Finally, there are only 24-hours in a day -- and workers need to rest. These are just a few illustrations of the scarcity of resources, items that are available in finite amounts. It is because these resources are available in finite amounts it constrains production, limiting the availability of goods and services.

Wherever and whenever wants exceed the supply of demanded goods or services, there is scarcity. Scarcity is tied in directly with cost and choice in that the more scarce something is, the more expensive it is. Therefore, common sense tells us the harder things are to find, or the more difficult they are to produce, the more expensive they will be. If diamonds were as common as quartz, no one would pay so much for such tiny amounts. Diamonds are scarce, they require capital intensive operations to mine and highly skilled labor to cut, polish and mount. For these reasons, a one carat diamond (200 milligrams) is relatively expensive.

Imagine if everyone in the world demanded steak every day. There are only so many cows in the world, only so many butchers, only so many beef processing plants, and only so many hours in a day to process the meat. There are only so many trucks, and stores to deliver and distribute the steak. In other words, it would be impossible to meet the demand. Even if the scope was limited to everyone in the United States demanding beef every single day, it would not be long before there would be no cows left in the world. This same example could be applied to anything. Unrestrained demand for any product or service would result in the exhaustion of the raw material or product.

Economizing is finding a solution to the problem of "using or administering scarce resources (the means of production) so as to attain the greatest or maximum fulfillment of society's unlimited wants (the goal of producing)." (Economics, Principles, Problems, and Policies, 8th ed.; C. R. McConnell, 1981.) There are five fundamental questions related to the economizing problem. What level should resources be utilized? What collection of goods and services will most fully satisfy society's wants-- i.e., what should be produced and how much? How should the output be produced, and what is the best combination of resources? How should the output of the economy be shared among the various economic units? Finally, can the economic system adapt and make changes to remain efficient over time?

The scarcity of economic resources is behind all of these questions. These fundamental questions are interrelated and do not exist in isolation. The level of the utilization of resources directly effects society. For human resources, there is a trade-off between work and leisure. More work means more pay but less time to enjoy the fruits of the labor. In relation to property resources, rapid exploitation of non-renewable natural resources would produce large output now, but leave nothing for later. Conservation is important so that future production is possible. Other choices effect the quality of our resources in the future. If some resources are not allocated for research and development, there would be no innovation, and no technological advances, limiting gains in efficiency. Possibly the most difficult of these questions relate to the ability to adapt to changing market conditions. This fundamental question is directly related to consumer tastes, changes in technology and the supply of resources. The inability of businesses to accommodate change leads to inefficiencies and stunts the growth of society as a whole.

Since it is impossible to satisfy all of society's material wants, what is attempted is to achieve the maximum possible satisfaction of these wants through efficiency -- efficiency in the use of scarce resources. Economic efficiency is concerned with both inputs and outputs, the relationship between the units of resources put into the process of production and the output of some desired product. Society wants to use scarce resources efficiently, to get the maximum amount of goods and services out of the limited resources available. In order to do this, there must be full employment and full production.

Full employment means that everyone who is willing and able to work has a job. In addition, full employment means that all available resources are put to use. Plants and arable land should not sit idle. Full production means that all resources should be used efficiently so that whatever is used is used to its maximum potential. Restated, it is the optimization of resources so that each resource contributes the most to total output. People should have jobs suited to their abilities so they can use their talents and add the most to the total output.

Even in a full employment, full production environment, it is still not possible to have an unlimited output of goods and services. This creates a problem in society because not everyone can have everything they want. It is for this reason several economic goals have been established that are widely accepted in our society. In order to solve the problem of scarcity and to attain efficiencies, the policies are centered around economic growth, full employment, price stability, economic freedom, and equitable distribution of income and economic security. (Economics, Principles, Problems, and Policies, 8th ed., C. R. McConnell, 1981). Some of these goals conflict and overlap, so our government and policy makers attempt to prioritize these goals. Central to the decision of what priority each objective takes is the economic cycle. Often that determines which political party gets elected and what policies are enacted.

During the Bush Presidency, tax rates were lowered on the wealthiest individuals, tax rates on capital gains and dividends were reduced and the very wealthy were able to keep more of their money. At the same time, real wages for middle class and lower class workers did not increase, nor did they benefit enough from reduced tax rates to maintain their standard of living. On Election Day, Americans overwhelmingly chose to repudiate the fiscal policies of the Republican Party. Voting in a Democratic President and majorities in Congress, people believed, would lead to economic policies that are more beneficial to society.

The priorities, with this election, has shifted from economic freedom to equitable distribution and economic security. This was a value judgment made by the people as a result of economic conditions. (Political Control of the Economy, E. R. Tufte, 1978.) It is the economic policy of our government to establish and maintain a stable growth rate in order to achieve full employment and full production. Even with the value judgments made and the policy changes being phased in, the outcome and effects on the problems in society are yet to be determined. Yet, the ultimate goals are still the same.

In order to analyze the effect of choices that must be made in society, one can refer to a simplified production possibility table. (Paul A. Samulson, Economics, 11th ed., 1980). The economizing problem requires several assumptions. First, it assumes that an economy is operating at full employment and full production. Second, that the supplies of the factors of production are fixed. They can be reallocated within limits, but not added to or reduced. Also, it must be assumed that the state of technology is fixed, that there are no technological advances. In other words, this is a pure "snapshot" of a specific period of time. Finally, to make this simpler, it is assumed that the economy only produces two products: bullets and bread. Bread represents consumer goods, items that directly satisfy the wants of the consumer.

In this scenario, society is faced with a choice -- with the total supply of resources limited, the total amount of bread and bullets that can be produced is also limited. What is the right amount of bread that should be made versus bullets? Because of full employment and full production, an increase in the production of bullets means less bread being made and vice-versa. Without bullets, the country may not be safe, without bread, the country may starve -- how do we choose the optimum ratio of bullets to bread?

PRODUCT PRODUCTION ALTERNATIVES

A	B	C	D	E
0	1	2	3	4
10	9	7	4	0

BREAD (1M LOAVES)
BULLETS (1M ROUNDS) 10

In order to satisfy society the most (At Level E), there is a cost. The country must sacrifice it's national security. In order to maximize its national security, the country must deny society of it's wants and needs. In the real world, an equilibrium must be found that balances the wants and needs of society with the ability to defend our nation. If one or the other is ignored, society will falter. The proper balance is to sacrifice some material wants and needs so that there can be a defense of our nation, which will allow future production of bread (consumer goods) later.

During ordinary times, this type of model could be used to generally gauge the effect of one policy choice over another. However, these are not ordinary times. Massive government intervention in response to a steep economic recession has led us to the possibility of unintended consequences. Society is beset by very high unemployment and very low production levels, resulting in a downward spiral of economic activity. Using the above production possibility table, everything is skewed to the negative and neither the maximum amounts of "bread" or "bullets" (or anything else for that matter) are being produced.

It is because of the unemployment and underemployment that our government has taken such drastic steps. It is an attempt to end the cycle of less jobs, less people making money, less demand for goods and services, leading to less manufacturing and even fewer jobs. It was the

Great Depression in the 1930's that undermined the classic theory of unemployment in a capitalistic system. Until then, it was argued that the price systems were capable of dealing with down cycles and provide for full employment.

It was then believed, under the Classical Economic Theory, that underspending was unlikely to occur and if that happened, changes in prices and wages would insure that declines in spending would not cause declines in real output, employment and real wages. This was based on "Say's Law", supply creates its own demand.

The Great Depression proved that to be untrue, as have many recessions since then. What the classic model failed to account for, as pointed out by John Maynard Keynes in his work, General Theory of Employment, Interest, and Money, was that the problem of unemployment can be brought about by the failure of fundamental economic decisions. Things such as interest rates, savings rates and investment decisions have the capacity to internally effect the economy.

Keynsian Economics, what is relied on today, pointed out that capitalism does not have self-regulating mechanisms and cannot be relied upon to run itself. In other words, reduced spending by consumers coupled with an increased savings rate, full-employment in equilibrium with maximum output can only happen by chance. Therefore, the problem of society seeking full employment and maximum output can only be resolved by accepting the correlation with demand. "The amount of goods and services produced, and therefore the level of employment, depend directly on the level of total spending or 'aggregate demand'." (C. R. McConnell, Id.)

The assumption that by simply producing more, demand would follow was soundly defeated.

What Keynsian Economics determined was that businesses will produce the level of output which they can profitably sell. As demand for goods and services fall, so too will the employment rate, production rate, and growth rate. Employment and productivity are inextricably tied to demand. The level at which scarce resources are deployed depends directly on the level of total spending. The circular flow between output and income dictate the utilization of the means of production as a function of demand and demand exerts its influence through the competitive pricing system.

Demand, which drives the allocation level of resources, directly effects the elements of the means of production. The full utilization of the different means of production: land, labor, capital, and entrepreneurial ability, are the components the demand of the consumer alters through spending. Everything that fuels our economy relies on these means of production and, therefore, they form the backbone of our system.

The four material resources can be further classified into two categories: property resource and human resources. Property resources refers to land and capital. "Land" refers to all natural resources as, "free gifts of nature," that are used in the productive process. (Economics, Principles, Problems, and Policies, 8th ed.; C. R. McConnell, 1981.) In this definition, used by economists, "land" includes arable land, minerals, forests, and water resources. Land is a necessity for any business. Beyond the standard understanding of this term, which simply implies a place to operate the business, land in this context is much broader. It is the area used for agriculture and forests, but it is also the water, oil, coal, natural gas, iron and many other raw materials used as the basis for producing goods. Without these vital elements of production, there would be no output. There would be no material to create products.

"Capital" is defined as manufactured aids to production such as tools, machinery or equipment; along with the factory, storage and transportation that enable the production of goods and services and get them to the ultimate consumer. (Id.) The usage of the term "capital" in this context does not include money, since money -- in and of itself -- does not produce anything. Instead, when discussing resources, "capital" is what is used to produce the goods that satisfy the needs of consumers. The factory provides a place to manufacture goods; tools and equipment are used to make the goods -- and it is through machinery that many efficiencies are created. Technological advances are usually implemented through machinery and new production techniques come into play within the sphere of an operation. If there was no place to create the goods or provide the services, there would be a very limited economy. If there ware no machines, no tools, many items that are produced today would not exist. Without storage, goods could only be produced on an "as needed" basis.

Unable to build up and store an inventory, shortages would result. Finally, without modes of transportation, there would be no way to obtain needed resources, nor deliver finished products to consumers. This would limit the availability of goods by geography and prevent growth, thwarting the expansion of markets. Lack of the means of transportation would hamper national and international trade. These are all necessary components of a vibrant economy.

The second category of the means of production, human resources, is often referred to as "labor." One element of human resources is entrepreneurial ability. Labor is best described as people's physical and mental talents used in the production of goods and services. Entrepreneurial ability, or enterprise, in economic terms, receives a more expanded consideration because of its special place in the capitalist system.

The entrepreneur acts as a driving force that brings the resources of land, capital and labor together in the production of goods and services. To the entrepreneur falls the task of making the policy decisions that sets the course of businesses. These enterprises are the innovators, the ones who create new processes, new technologies and try to find way of generating profits. Entrepreneurs take on the risk, putting their income and savings to work in business ventures that have no guarantee of success. The investments into new enterprises are catalysts for increased efficiencies, more competition and technological advances. Because of the time, effort, money, and special skills, entrepreneurial ability commands an economic premium. Success in these terms means generating a profit.

The necessity of these risk-takers in our economy cannot be overstated. It is the ability to make new and better products, to push the edge of technology, and to implement new methods of production that has propelled this nation forward so quickly.

The exchange of these resources to businesses is done for money or income. Payment is made for the transfer of ownership of land or raw materials. Wages, salaries, commissions and bonuses are paid for labor. Payments made for usage of property or capital equipment is made in interest or rental fees. For the entrepreneur, the income received is called profits. The payment for the use of the factors of production is what provides the stimulus for further demand, further production or further innovation.

All of the means of production are necessary in order for a business to be a functioning concern. In our society, the businesses that produce goods and services create the demand for the means of production, meaning there is an economic cost involved in procuring what is needed to create the products. In the marketplace for land, labor, capital and entrepreneurial ability, the scarcity of resources dictate the cost. However, a sometimes opposing counterforce exists. Economic efficiency is created by obtaining a given output of a product using the smallest input of these resource in terms of dollars and cents. Contrary to the demands of labor, a business wants to pay as little as possible for labor. On the other hand, they are willing to pay more for specialized talents and abilities. The needs of the business for labor and the demand for payment for the work finds an equilibrium in the market for jobs.

Although all of the means of production are required in order to produce goods, labor's spending of the income derived from their work seems to make the worker the most significant component. This is borne out by the functional distribution of income. When society's money is divided among wages, rent, interest and profits, the lion's share goes to labor. The personal distribution of income is how the money is apportioned amongst individual households.

A person's physical skills and mental abilities which are used in the production of goods and services are subject to the laws of supply and demand, as are all commodities. A more skilled worker will expect and secure more income than an unskilled worker. Without the knowledge and ability to create products, there would be no production, regardless of the availability of raw materials or capital. It is labor who creates the supply of goods and services. But it is also labor who demands the supply of goods and service. It is for this reason that the bulk of income goes to labor and not capital.

The personal distribution of income is a major determinate of the size and composition of what is ultimately produced. It is also a factor in how society divides its money between consumption and savings. Consumption is the driving force behind output and employment in our economy. A highly unequal distribution of income results in a greater demand for and output of luxury goods. The economy shifts and the change in product mix determines how the country's resources are used.

These market forces also apply to the quest for land, and the want of newer, more efficient capital. Suppliers of these resources want to maximize their profits even as the businesses seek to keep costs down. The key to maximum efficiency in the derived demand market is competition.

Another reason the means of production are important is how the cost is related to supply. Land, labor, capital and entrepreneurial ability are scarce resources, and therefore have a price tag attached to them. There are several factors involved in determining the supply, or output, of a particular product. Price is the main component, but included in that are the technique of production (the technology used) and the total resource prices. Anything that serves to lower the production cost will increase the supply. With lower costs of resources, or better technology, businesses will find it profitable to offer a larger amount of the product at each possible price. Conversely, an increase of the cost of resources will raise costs and cause a decrease in supply.

It is competition which forces firms to adopt the most efficient production techniques. Failing to use the least costly production techniques usually leads to failure as other competing firms push them out of business. Businesses use the least costly combination of resources in producing a given output because it is in their own self interest to do so. It is also a societal interest to maximize efficiencies, in that to do otherwise would sacrifice resources that could be put to better use. The competitive pricing system guides these resources into the production of goods and services most wanted by consumers.

The cost of production translates into money income (wages and salaries) for labor, rent income and interest income for capital, and payments for raw materials, and profits for the enterprise. The money income derived from payment by businesses translates into demand for other goods and services by the workforce and entrepreneurs. This is the nexus between economizing and the means of production. It is this connection that makes full employment and full production so important in our society.

The means of production are also related to possible market failures. Market failures are when the competitive pricing system either produces the wrong amount of goods or services; or, fail to allocate any resources to certain goods or services whose output is economically justified. The first situation results in spillovers and the second involves "public" or "social" goods.

A spillover occurs when some of the benefits or costs associated with the production of a good or service "spill over" to third parties. This spillover could be negative (a cost) or positive (benefit). An example of a spillover cost would be pollution. The public suffers from toxic air or water and the firm creating it does not account for the cost of that debasement of natural resources in the cost of production. If there were pollution controls in place, that would be an added expense -- adding to the actual cost of production. Instead, society pays the price with their health, or through government clean-ups of toxic waste sites. The destruction of natural resources, such as tainted land, foul water and poisoned fish, goes unaccounted for, but continue to harm society and create a negative economic impact.

An example of a spillover benefit would be education. Education provides benefits to individuals consumers because higher educated people generally earn higher incomes than less educated individuals. However, education also benefits society and has a direct impact on the means of production. The economy as a whole benefits from a more versatile workforce. Countries with a work force with higher levels of education tend to be more productive and more efficient. There are other societal spillover benefits from education including lower crime rates, smaller layouts for law enforcement and less welfare payments. There is no way to quantify the exact level of spillover benefits from education but it can be said that the market failure is that society underallocates resources to this commodity.

Public goods are goods and services that would not be created or provided at all given the competitive pricing system in place in our society. As opposed to private goods, these "social" products cannot be divided up and sold in units, nor can anyone be excluded from partaking of them once they are produced. A classic example of a public good is a lighthouse. In a dangerous harbor, its benefits are obvious and justified, and it is helpful to all ships -- so the benefits do not accrue to any single user. Because there can be no economic benefit derived from building the lighthouse, it would be unprofitable for a business to use its resources to build it. They cannot selecively choose who sees the light, and thus cannot charge a fee. Hence, the government steps in and, using taxpayer's money, provides a public good.

In instances like this, it is a collective choice to allocate the necessary resources and they are a matter of public policy. The effects choices like these have on the means of production are not only the reallocation of resources, but the draining effect of taxation. If there are too many public goods produced, (be it schools, highways, military hardware) that would require higher taxes to pay for them. Higher taxes would result in lower income for the consumers. Taxes tend to diminish private demand for goods and service, and this decrease in turn prompts a drop in the private demand for resources. In short, Government purposefully reallocates resources to bring about changes in the composition of the economy's total output.

Another connection between the allocation of means of production, especially labor, and the supply of products is the amount of household incomes. There are several determinants that effect how much each household makes. The first is the quantities of various human and property resources a household is able and willing to supply to businesses. Another factor is the prices which these resources command in the resource market. Finally, there is the actual level of employment of these resources. Most households only supply labor services as a resource to business, wherein they derive their money income. However, that leaves them subject to the willingness of businesses to utilize their labor. There is no guarantee that firms will be willing to pay for each person's labor. Within the business cycle, this solidifies why full-employment is so important to our economy.

Full employment, in the real world, does not mean 100% employment. There are factors such as part-time workers, people between jobs, discouraged workers and bad information that makes the actual unemployment rate difficult to determine. Because of these factors, called frictional unemployment, full employment is considered to be something less than 100%. Even with the difficulties of quantifying the actual rate, the significant point to make is the overall effect on the economy. Unemployment exacts a great social and economic cost on society.

The basic economic cost of unemployment is lost output. When the economy fails to generate enough jobs for all who are willing and able to work, potential production of goods and services is forever forfeited. History has shown that severe unemployment has been the cause of sometimes violent social and political unrest. It is the attempt to avoid these catastrophic upheavals that is the driving force behind economic policy. With no work and no money, people are unable to satisfy their wants and needs.

Everything circles back to the central facts of economics, society's material wants are virtually unlimited, and economic resources are limited, or scarce. Scarcity of products and the means of production are dictated by price, price is a function of supply and demand. Supply and demand are determined by the fundamental questions of economizing. And, the solutions to society's problems, i.e., how to derive the most satisfaction using the fewest resources relate back to the level of utilization of the means of production. The four elements of the means of production form the backbone of the economic system and efficient utilization of those resources is effected by competition and Government. Full employment and full production leads to the demand of more products and resources, thus spurring growth and a continuation of the economic cycle.

DEFINING AND DELINEATING ECONOMIC SECTORS

The American Economy

The American economy can be divided into several sectors. The first demarcation line is the private sector versus the public sector. In the private sector, further distinctions can be made, revealing a broad spectrum of operating structures of businesses and diverse functionality. Through several different business platforms, various methods are used to obtain financing and manage the operation of businesses. The public sector, or governments; be it federal, state or local, operate much differently. Because of its magnitude, there is much more complexity. However, at the most basic level, the economic operation of every government entity boils down to taxing, borrowing and spending -- the reallocation of resources intended to meet the needs of the people.

The interaction with other nations through imports and exports provides the economy with many benefits. However, there are many potential pitfalls as well. The economic sector dealing with international trade has grown significantly over the years. Obtaining the maximum benefit from international commerce while limiting adverse situations, depends upon many factors. Governments and businesses must work, together in order to accommodate international trade. Treaties and trade agreements are necessary to try and secure fair trade between nations.

In the mixed-market economy practiced in the United States, businesses make up the second largest aggregate after households. Enterprises in the private sector utilize several forms, in accordance with business laws and accounting rules, so as to achieve efficiencies and provide transparency for accurate financial reporting. Management decisions, profit distribution, taxation along with many choices made by businesses depend upon how an enterprise is organized.

Businesses organize and find funding (or capitalize) in several different ways. Sole proprietorships, partnerships and corporations are the three major legal forms which business enterprises may assume. Each one has a different ownership structure and they use different methods of operation, which convey different advantages and disadvantages.

Sole proprietorships account for the largest number of businesses in the United States. A proprietorship literally means someone in business for themselves. He or she is the sole owner and operator of that business and is fully responsible for its success or failure. The proprietor owns or obtains all of the necessary capital equipment and materials used for operation and makes all of the decisions to efficiently utilize the means of production.

The advantages of a sole proprietorship are many. It is easy to organize and there are few legal requirements. There is also less costs involved in establishing a business as a proprietorship. The proprietor is his or her own boss and has freedom of action. Finally, the profits, based upon the success of the venture, belong solely to the owner. That creates a strong motivation, a powerful incentive to make wise business decisions.

There are also disadvantages in establishing a business as a sole proprietorship. In the majority of cases, the financial resources of a sole proprietor are limited. Funding for all operations can only come from one source and that limits the growth potential of even a successful business. It is possible to borrow money to expand, but lending institutions may not be willing to provide funding to an individual who may not be around when the time comes to repay the loan. When a sole proprietor dies, usually, so does the business. Banks see that as a risk and hesitate to make large, long-term loans to sole proprietorships.

Another disadvantage is the responsibility of managing and being responsible for every aspect of the operation. Many of the sub-specialties of business operations are unavailable to the sole proprietor. He or she must fill every role and is responsible for every aspect of the business.

Finally, and most significantly, operating a business as a sole proprietor subjects the owner to unlimited liability. Not only is their business responsible for any claims against it, the owners themselves are personally responsible for those claims. That puts the personal assets of the owner at risk from creditors and as such, they can lose everything.

A partnership is a natural extension of a proprietorship. Instead of one owner, there are two or more owners. Direct control of the enterprise can be shared among the partners depending on the arrangement agreed upon at the formation of the partnership. This structure is meant to overcome some of the shortcomings of a sole proprietorship. The partners pool their resources, making more capital available. This means they share the risk along with the profits and losses of the business venture.

There are a vast number of possible combinations or variations of partnerships and their business structures. Some partners may contribute equally in financing and business acumen, other partnerships may include silent partners who stay out of the day to day operations, yet participate in profits after contributing investment capital. Like a sole proprietorship, partnerships can be easy to establish and cost less to start. Frequently based on written agreements, legal red-tape involved in starting a partnership is usually at a minimum. Beyond any state and local licensing fees or permits, there are very few expenses involved in establishing a business organized as a partnership.

Because there is more than one owner, another advantage is that the responsibilities and specialized talents involved in running a business can be spread out among the two or several owners. Another advantage over a proprietorship is that there are more resources to draw from, possibly more money available to expand and grow the operation.

However, there are more problems involved in partnerships. The division of management and responsibilities can lead to disagreements or inconsistency in business operations. Unless specifically defined at the onset of the business, distribution of profits can also lead to contention.

Even with partners, the availability of financing is still limited in most instances. Additionally, there is no guarantee the partnership will survive. The death or withdrawal of a partner usually leads to dissolution of the business. Because of the potential mortality of the business, banks deem loans to partnerships a risky proposition.

Partnerships suffer from the same unattractive legal status as proprietorships -- that is to say, unlimited liability for the partners. The partners, not just the business, are personally responsible for any claims against the business. That liability extends to the actions of other partners and their business decisions. The wealthiest partner takes on the greatest personal risk, no matter what his stake is in the business.

Corporations are much different than both the sole proprietorship and the partnership. A corporation is a legal entity, separate and distinct from the people who own them. As such, businesses are deemed "legal persons" under the law. Functioning with that legal status allows corporations to hold titles to properties, enter contracts, acquire resources, retain assets, sell products, incur debt, and do anything a person or other type of business platform can do.

The organizational structure of a corporation can take on numerous forms. When setting up a corporation, the incorporators must set up a charter and a set of bylaws. The charter includes the name of the proposed corporation, the type of activities it will pursue, the amount of capital stock, the number of directors, and the names and addresses of the directors. The charter is then filed with the secretary of the state where the corporation plans to have headquarters. Once approved, the corporation comes into existence.

The bylaws are the rules drawn up by the founders of the corporation. They set out the internal management of the company. Included in those rules are how the directors are elected, whether existing shareholders have the first rights to buy any new shares if they are issued, provisions for establishing committees and their duties, and procedures for changing the bylaws themselves. Establishing a corporation requires much more paperwork, and probably assistance from a lawyer. Along with registration fees to the state, it is more expensive to start a corporation than the other business platforms, but is worth it in the long run.

There are major advantages in establishing a business as a corporation. The primary benefit is that the owners of the corporation have limited liability. In other words, the owners (shareholders) risk only the amount they paid for the stock they purchased in the corporation. Creditors cannot demand repayment of loans made to the corporation from the owners. Those who own the shares are not personally responsible for the liabilities of the corporation. Limited liability reduces the risk to investors, which makes the business more valuable.

Another major advantage of the corporation is the ability to raise money. Capital, the money necessary to purchase assets, grow and expand, is readily available through the sale of stocks (equity) and bonds (taking on debt). Thousands upon thousands of individuals can invest in a corporation through buying an ownership stake (buying stock) or loaning the corporation money (buying bonds). The ability to raise money allows for better growth opportunities. The ability to grow adds even more value to a business because there is a greater potential for increased profits. The shareholders participate in the profits while not having to worry about the day to day management of the business.

Because the corporation is a "legal entity" its life continues beyond the lives of the owners. In a legal sense, corporations are immortal, barring dissolution through bankruptcy. Because of this longevity, independent of the founders or owners, it enables long-term planning. It is less risky for institutions to loan corporations money because there is expected continuity of an ongoing concern.

As opposed to proprietorships and partnerships, corporations are more capable of hiring people who specialize in specific business tasks. This is simply a function of having more money available to operate. The ability to hire people who focus on different aspects of the business spreads out the responsibility and allows more efficient management of specific elements of the business. This is opposed to one or several people being responsible for every single aspect of an operation, facets where they may have no training or experience.

Corporations are taxed differently than sole proprietorships and partnerships. In many instances, tax laws favor corporations. In proprietorships and partnerships, profits are taxed as personal income. In certain circumstances, corporations can take advantage of the tax laws and pay a much lower rate. Because of these advantages, and since most firms are managed with value maximization in mind, the greatest volume of business is conducted by corporations.

Organizing A Business

There are some drawbacks to organizing a business as a corporation. Paramount is the legal red-tape involved in setting up and maintaining a corporation. There are legal expenses and accounting expenses above and beyond those of proprietorships or partnerships. There are regulatory and reporting requirements that must be met on a quarterly basis (every three months).

Because ownership of a corporation is so diffuse, possibly tens to hundreds of thousands of shareholders, there can be dissatisfaction from the minority shareholders. They may not like the way a business is being run or may object to business decisions. But, because they do not control a majority of the outstanding shares, they have little to no say about how the business is run. Typical shareholders rarely vote when the opportunity arises. More activist shareholders may vote but may not be able to garner the support to challenge the board of directors. Without direct control, minority shareholders may not approve of decisions and that creates friction between management and the owners.

A prime example of the divisions that may cause friction is the decision about what to do with profits. Does the company pay out profits in the form of dividends? Or, does the company retain the earning, adding capital, to grow or expand into other business ventures? Some may want dividends while the directors may see other opportunities to increase value.

Possible double-taxation is another disadvantage inherent to corporations. As an entity, the business is taxed at the corporate rate. Upon distributions of dividends, the owners of the company, the shareholders, are taxed personally. This negative aspect must be weighed against the fact that corporations pay taxes at a lower rate than proprietorships and partnerships.

There is one final shortcoming of corporations which comes from the social perspective. The corporate form of enterprise has the potential for abuse. Unscrupulous managers or owners can use the legal status of a corporation for questionable practices while avoiding personal responsibility. Despite legislation to curtail fraud and government agencies tasked with preventing abuse, corporations all too often have engaged in selling worthless securities to the public. Also, directors and managers sometimes take advantage of their positions within a corporation for personal gain. This potential for abuse and the use of corporations to shield individuals from responsibility is not an inherent defect. It is just a possible occurrence we have seen much too often lately.

Corporations benefit from the fact that through the issuance of shares, ownership is easily transferred from one person to another. Having the ability to quickly buy and sell these shares increases the willingness of people to invest in companies because they are not "stuck" in an ownership position they may no longer want to be in. Stock exchanges provide liquidity (the ability to sell shares) by making markets in those securities and matching up buyers and sellers.

In a corporation, ownership is spread out among many shareholders. However, it is the established (or elected) board of directors who makes the big decisions. Shareholders vote on who gets elected to the board, but the hiring and placement of management and other critical decisions are mostly out of the hands of the minority shareholders. It is usually the founders of the corporation who retain the most shares. With the majority stake in the ownership, they control the board, thus controlling the business.

However, shares in many major corporations are so well distributed that the many small shareholders collectively choose who will run the business. No matter the structure or who controls what percentage of ownership, those who sit on the board have a fiduciary responsibility to act for the benefit of all shareholders.

In order to better understand a corporation, it is necessary to define "capital" as it relates to the formation and continuing operation of a corporation. In order to operate, a business must have assets. In order to acquire assets, the business must start with capital, or money. Capital can be raised in two forms, either through issuing debt securities or selling equity. There are many types of debt a corporation can take on, and there are various forms of equity.

Corporate debt may be long-term, short-term, interest bearing, non-interest bearing, secured or unsecured. A very common form of a debt security is a bond. A corporation issues bonds and sells them to the individuals, governments, other businesses or financial institutions. Bonds are simply promissory notes that have a face value (called a par value), usually pays a set interest rate, and have a maturity date. The buyers of the bonds are lending money to corporations in return for the interest payments (paid out at regular intervals) and then, at maturity, repayment of the face value of the bond.

Equity is represented by preferred stock and common stockholder's equity. Common equity includes both paid-in capital and retained earnings. "Paid-in capital" represents the money paid for ownership shares (common stock) of the corporation. The more shares of stock a person owns, the higher the percentage of ownership they retain. The paid-in capital exchanged for those shares is the financing used to purchase assets and operate the business. In return for the capital, the common shareholders are the owners of the corporation and they retain certain rights and privileges.

"Retained earnings" is the money a corporation has saved and accumulated from its earnings since the company started operations. The retained earnings are in addition to the paid-in capital under shareholders' equity. These funds are used to buy more assets or fund operations.

Financial institutions and stock exchanges make up the financial markets that are tasked with providing and maintaining liquidity for the equity (stocks) and debt (bonds) issued by corporations. It is through these institutions and markets that corporations and governments raise capital. A secure, regulated environment in the these markets is necessary to maintain investor confidence. Otherwise, people and other institutions would be hesitant to risk their investment dollars by investing in illiquid or possibly fraudulent securities. A healthy economy depends upon efficient transfer of money from savers to corporations who need capital. These transfers must also be low-cost as well.

For these reasons, the various financial markets are highly regulated and there are reporting requirements that must be met by every corporation. As seen in the financial crisis on late 2008 and into 2009, absent market stability, confidence, transparency or security, the credit markets (dealing with debt) froze up and the equity markets (dealing with stocks) collapsed.

The result has been a crisis in our economy, resulting in a recession because corporations could not raise capital to fund operations. The lack of faith in the financial markets made the cost of borrowing money prohibitively expensive, even as interest rates were at historic lows.

The additional cost at that time was a "risk" premium corporations would have had to pay to someone willing to lend them money. At the same time, the valuation of corporate stocks fell dramatically, making the sale of additional equity very unattractive at such low prices.

The net effect of corporations' inability to raise capital was cost-cutting through reduction of staff and less production. Higher unemployment meant less demand for goods and services offered by corporations. This spiraling effect had broad implications, affecting every sector, and the economy as a whole. The Gross National Product shrunk precipitously in the last quarter of 2008 and the first quarter of 2009.

Because the credit markets were frozen and the impact that was having on the private sector, it was necessary for the federal government to take drastic steps in order to stabilize the economy. Not just in the United States, but globally, governments have intervened through spending programs and mass capital injections into financial institutions. Parts of the private sector have thus become reliant on the public sector for its survival.

Stabilization Function

Probably the most important aspect of government as it relates to the economy is the stabilization function. Assisting the private sector to achieve both full employment of resources and stable prices has taken on a greater, continually growing role since the Great Depression. The intervention into the markets through capital injections in late 2008 and early 2009 is said by many economists to have staved off another depression. Because the level of output (production) depends directly on total spending or aggregate demand, the federal government used many tools and financial resources to pump money into the economy. The government made more money available to the private sector and averted a more severe crisis.

It was only through these actions that the credit markets began to function, making capital available to financial institutions for them to lend to corporations. This slowed the rate of declining productivity in the private sector and leveled off the number of workers being fired. It has become the government's obligation in a mixed-market economy to augment private demand so that total demand (both public and private) is sufficient to generate full employment. Another method used to do this has been to increase spending.

The economic functions of government beyond stabilization are many, and they are quite varied. The role of government is so broad in scope, it would be virtually impossible to delineate every aspect. The financial bailouts used to help the economy recover show the vast power and reach of the government. The public sector, in one way or another, has a direct impact on every household, business and the economy. Federal, state and local governments comprise the public sector and through taxes, fees, fines and other facilities, take in revenues. Through spending, they redistribute wealth and provide services in an attempt to meet the needs of the people.

It is the government who establishes the legal framework and social environment that enables a fluid economy. Through laws, regulations, control of the currency, and influence on interest rates, the public sector helps maintain competition, protects rights, modifies the price system, enables trade and adjusts the allocation of resources. Through tax policy, spending, public programs, and fiscal policy, governments redistribute wealth, stabilizes the economy, and promote economic growth. Along with these functions, all forms of governments provide vital services that private enterprises are unable or unwilling to do. These services also have a direct economic impact.

The legal foundation that sustains this country's economy serves a vital role. Some examples include: protection of property rights, business securities regulation, antitrust laws, consumer protection, environmental protection, labor and fair employment practices, protection of intellectual property rights, enforcement of contracts, and a system of conflict resolution. Without the public sector laying out the "rules of the game" there would not be a stable economy. These rules allow for the effective operation of a market economy.

The public sector provides for the services that encourage a secure environment for the private sector. The government uses police powers to maintain internal order. Also, they provide standards of weights and measures for better trade and commerce. They regulate the quality of certain products to insure safety. They establish and regulate the monetary system. Nationally, they fund the military for the protection of the people, property and rights of this nation. On the state and local level, for example, some communities or agencies provide trash collection, water and sewer services, and regulate natural gas and electricity. Local governments regulate what types of businesses can be established and where. Most schools and hospitals also fall under the state and local realm of control and financing. All of these, and more, are functions of the public sector.

In a market economy, government plays a major role in insuring competition. Since competition in the private sector is the main regulatory mechanism in a capitalistic system, the government has passed laws and has established agencies in order to prevent and curtail monopolistic practices. It is important to allow prices to be set by supply and demand and that entails making sure there are many suppliers. This is vital function of government because monopolies alter the economy as a whole in drastic, negative ways.

The government plays an active role in redistributing wealth because the distribution of income in the capitalistic system may entail more inequality than society desires. Simply put, in our society, no one wants to see people starving in the streets because they are too old to work and have no resources, or someone cannot find a job. The market economy provides very high incomes to those with special skills, abilities or education and training. Also, those who inherit vast resources are able to benefit greatly by putting those resources to work through investments. Others, who are not so fortunate, or who did not benefit from a decent education or training, earn very low wages. Add in the handicapped, the infirm, the elderly, and disadvantaged minorities, and poverty is a huge problem.

Government has taken on the responsibility of attempting to alter the unequal distribution of wealth through social programs. Public assistance, or welfare, provides for the needy. Social Security and Medicare provide for the elderly. These programs bring income to households who would otherwise have little to none. This, in turn, allows people who would otherwise have nothing to buy goods and services. That also helps the private sector because there are more consumers of goods.

Furthermore, the government can also effect market prices of some goods and services through market intervention. Setting price supports for farmers and setting a minimum wage are examples of price fixing that alters the free market forces in the private sector and alters the economy.

To do all the things a government does costs money. In order to get the revenue necessary to function and meet the demands of the people, the government imposes taxes. That is their main source of revenue. There are additional sources, but taxation is the primary vehicle of raising revenue. On the federal level, the government imposes personal income taxes and corporate income taxes. They also collect contributions to fund Social Security and other social programs. On the state level, most states have a sales tax, most states also levy an income tax on individuals and corporations. Locally, the main source of revenue is property taxes. The degree of state and local taxation varies from location to location as well as other fees, surcharges and many other methods states and localities use to raise revenues.

The federal income tax is designed to take a greater proportion of the incomes of the rich and a lesser proportion from the poor. State income tax policy can vary from following the same model as the federal government to having no income tax at all, relying on sales taxes instead.

Local governments, municipalities, establish their own tax policy. Through such wide variations from town to town, they have unintentionally created pockets of great wealth and pockets of severe poverty across the nation.

All levels of the public sector seemingly have extended their reach into the pockets of households and businesses by instituting more and more taxes and fees in order to raise the money to pay for all of the projects, programs and services they provide or have promised. Giving and promising so much to the people, yet unable or unwilling to curtail spending in other areas has led to large yearly budget deficits and mounting debt. The appropriate size and function of the public sector is always a debatable subject.

Financing government operations and providing for programs has only been possible through borrowing money and/or raising taxes. At all levels of government, in order to pay for large capital projects, programs, or to make up for shortfalls in revenue, they have raised money through the sale of debt securities.

Government bonds function the same as corporate bonds in that they have a face (par) value, pay a set interest rate and promise repayment of the par value on the date of maturity. Governments or government agencies sell their bonds to all the other sectors. These bonds can take many forms, but government bonds simply represent loans to the different government entities.

Federal Debt Securities

Through the United States Treasury, the federal government sells long, medium and short-term debt securities. Not only are these bonds used to finance projects, functions and operations of the government, but they are also used to manipulate interest rates and monetary policy with the coordinated effort of the Federal Reserve.

The Congress of the United States controls spending and budgetary matters, which includes the level of debt the country, by law, is allowed to take on. The federal government spends most of its money on entitlements (social welfare programs) and national defense. Another large portion is committed to servicing the nation debt. After veteran's affairs, education, commerce and transportation, only a small percentage of federal spending is allocated for other projects. Relatively speaking, that small percentage is still a very large amount of money and many things are accomplished. Because of recent wars and the financial crisis that started in 2008, the level of spending has increased dramatically in many areas. This has forced the federal government to sell more bonds than ever to fund it all.

United States Government bonds, like other government and corporate bonds, trade freely on the open market where individuals, other governments, corporations and financial institutions can buy and sell these debt instruments. Backed by the full faith and credit of the United States, there is a near-zero risk of default on these bonds. This allows the government to sell their bonds at a very low interest rate, relative to the debt market as a whole. The effective yield on the Treasury bonds is the standard by which the pricing of all other bonds are set.

States and municipalities also sell bonds to the private sector and other governments. To encourage the purchase of municipal bonds, many states have conveyed a favorable tax status on the interest income provided by the bonds. And, because the bonds are backed by the credit of the states or localities, they also carry a very low risk of default. This enables states and municipalities to pay a very low interest rate on those bonds. The sale of these bonds allows for capital projects such as new roads, government buildings, hospitals, and schools. The payment of interest and repayment of principle of the bonds is done by raising revenue through taxation. Since bonds are also used to fill budget gaps, selling them also assists states with paying for services and public safety.

Local governments, who primarily collect revenue though property taxes, spend most of it on education. They are also responsible for paying for police, fire departments, housing, parks and sanitation. Local governments also support hospitals and must pay for the upkeep of local roads and highways. Like the federal and state governments, municipalities often have to borrow money in order to pay for all they do and have promised.

A final, but very important function of the federal government is to foster trade. Our economy is an open economy and because of advances in transportation, communication and technology, an ever growing part of our economy relates to international trade. The United States is linked to other nations through a complex series of trade and financial relationships. Imports and exports accounted for $3.2 trillion dollars of economic activity in the year 2000. Because this is such an important part of our economy, the public and private sector must work together in order to fully benefit from it. The government must make every effort to insure fair trade and optimize efficiencies for the private sector.

International trade is a way nations can specialize, increase productivity of their resources, and realize a greater total output. In other words, if one nation has the ability to produce goods more efficiently than another, they can trade those goods for other items they cannot produce efficiently. This is possible because the resources of the world are unevenly distributed and also each nation has its own specialized means of production.

The efficient production of goods requires the right combination or resources and technologies. For example, the United States is completely dependent upon other nations for certain commoditites and materials which cannot be obtained domestically. As stated by Adam Smith in The Wealth of Nations, "It is the maxim of every prudent master of a family, never to attempt to make at home what it will cost him more to make than to buy." (p. 424)

It is through free trade that the world can achieve a more efficient allocation of resources. Promulgating free trade, however, is difficult to establish and maintain. Trading partners have to exchange meaningful information pertaining to the wants, needs, capabilities and capacities of their economy. Rules of trade must be formulated. Through negotiated agreements, which result in fair trade, and more equitable import-export activity, an economy's private sector can prosper, which in turn creates more means for the public sector to redistribute. From the sole proprietorship to the major corporation to the federal government, trade increases opportunity and increases the utilization of resources.

A few of the barriers of free trade include protective tariffs and quotas. Tariffs are simply an excise tax on imported goods. They may be imposed for purposes of revenue or protection. The protective tariffs are designed to shield domestic producers from foreign competition. The additional cost raises the price of goods and puts the imported goods at a competitive disadvantage. Import quotas specify the maximum amounts of specific commodities which may be imported during a given period of time. Quotas are more effective in slowing international commerce because imports are prohibited once the quota is reached.

These government imposed tools to restrict trade are used for a variety of reasons: special interests, domestic stimulus, defense or industrialization are a few of those reasons. In order to advance free trade, the nations of the world have made several important agreements and have formed agencies to lower these barriers.

In 1947, many nations, including the United States, signed the General Agreement on Tariffs and Trade (GATT). GATT was based on three principles: equal, non-discriminatory treatment for all members; the reduction of tariffs by multilateral negotiations; and, the elimination of import quotas. GATT thus became the forum for the negotiation of reductions in tariff barriers between nations. More than 100 countries now participate in GATT and it has been an important force in the liberalization of trade between nations.

GATT promoted free trade by trying to reduce tariffs and quotas between nations. Also, it promoted fair trade by defining trade practices like unfair government subsidies for exports and "dumping." Dumping is selling goods far below fair market value in a foreign market. GATT also established panels to resolve trade disputes and work on settling issues such as intellectual property rights. Through the negotiations of the General

Agreement of Tariffs and Trade, the World Trade Organization (WTO) was formed. The WTO is an international economic organization that is intended to provide leadership and coordinate international trade.

The World Trade Organization was officially established in 1995 and is not just an extension of GATT. While GATT is simply an agreement between nations, the WTO is an organization with a formal structure, a staff and a budget. As of 2002, there were over 145 members of the World Trade Organization whose mission is to facilitate free trade and provide protections for not only a nation's material goods, but also services and intellectual rights. It is the WTO who monitors and has the authority to make decisions on any matters or disputes between nations which are based on recognized mutltilateral trade agreements.

There are many examples of trade agreements between nations that are recognized by the WTO. In Western Europe, there is the a free trade zone called the European Union. In the Americas, import and export between the United States, Canada and Mexico falls under NAFTA, the North American Free Trade Agreement. The establishment of the European Common Market and NAFTA eliminated tariffs between the member nations of those agreements. It also allowed for more fluid direct investments across boarders. Another significant change was that these agreements allowed workers to move more freely between nations to work.

The effect of these agreements on international trade has been to increase economic activity. The efficiencies permitted an increased level of trade, but that has had some unintended consequences. Some of these effects have benefited the private sector of our economy, some have been detrimental. For example, a corporation is able to have products manufactured more cheaply in under-developed nations because of lower wages. That is good for the corporation because it reduces the cost of production and allows for a higher profit margin. On the other hand, manufacturing jobs in the United States have been lost and many laborers forced out of work as their jobs have been shipped overseas.

The government, and parts of the private sector, have been slow to react to the economic realities that have come about with more liberal trade. Corporations will always seek to utilize the most efficient means of production. If building products is cheaper elsewhere, that is where businesses will go. Those in the private sector who are unable to adapt to the changing environment are left behind. No longer are workers able to depend upon increasing wages and benefits for low-skilled jobs their father's generation relied upon for lifetime security. Corporations can easily find cheaper labor on other shores, people who can and will work just as hard for magnitudes less.

The trouble in the auto industry is a prime example of an industry working against economic forces. It was the failure of those corporations to adapt to a global marketplace, the labor unions demanding exorbitant compensation, and the failure of government to intervene sooner--in such an important industry--that resulted in the collapse of two producers. For example, there was no justification for a corporation agreeing to pay and paying some laborers $40/hour to operate a pneumatic wrench--tightening bolts. That was the same rate iron foundry workers were paid. Comparatively speaking, someone doing that same low-skilled job in China would make $40 a day.

Once laid off, the American auto worker had no other skill set and, along with thousands of other workers in the auto sector, remain unemployed. Multiple factors contributed to the situation where building cars in America became much more expensive than cars built in Asia: wasteful spending by executives, poor planning, bad business decisions, union demands and unequal wages with trading partners are just a few. The public and private sectors must work together in order to alter the course of our economy.

The public sector, through incentives for better education, training, and investment in technology, along with demanding better terms of trade with other nations, could transform our economy.

The federal government must make policies that will raise the standard of living for the people in other countries, the households of our trading partners. By putting pressure on nations like China to allow the currency exchange rate to float, that would raise the purchasing power of the Chinese people. Also, wages for workers in other nations have to rise so that those people are able to purchase more goods imported from our country; and, so that our workers are on an more equal footing. Corporations will retain jobs within our borders if the wages paid domestically are not multiples above the wages of labor in other nations.

The private sector also has to do more to protect the livelihood of the labor force. Because the household sector is the most prolific spender in our economy, all forms of business actually do a disservice to themselves, and to the economy, by hoarding wealth or enabling a few executives or owners to accumulate a vast majority of the fruits of a profitable venture. A well compensated work-force creates more demand for all goods and services. In addition, allocating resources for better training and education would create a more efficient, adaptable, labor pool that would make a firm more competitive and better able to adjust when necessary.

Working together in our mixed-market economy, the public and the private sector can strengthen this nation. The sole proprietorships, partnerships and corporations, operate based on the principle of making money. They have the capacity to outclass many government functions in terms of efficiency. Exchanging a small portion of profitability in order to advance the capabilities of labor would increase labor's wage potential and would reduce some of the public sector's responsibilities.

For their part, governments have to incentivize education, better training, and advances in technologies. The transformation to a more self-sufficient population who has a greater ability to adapt would reduce the need for social programs, market intervention and wealth distribution--which in turn would lower spending. That would then enable goverenments to reduce the tax burden on individuals and corporations. Simultaneously, the government should take steps to make international trade more balanced. These steps would eventually reduce the role of the public sector and allow the marketplace controlled by the private sector to function more freely.

www.ingramcontent.com/pod-product-compliance
Lightning Source LLC
Chambersburg PA
CBHW021957170526
45157CB00003B/1036